KEEP
YOUR
FOCUS

ENDORSEMENTS

Senior leadership roles can be lonely – it can be difficult to ask for help when you are expected to have all the answers. Sarah has distilled years of scientific research and extensive executive coaching experience into practical insights that are directly relevant for all leaders. *Keep Your Focus* is an honest and intelligent read - and beautifully written to boot.

Sally Hutton, Managing Partner, Webber Wentzel

Sarah shared these "blogs" with me over years. I enjoyed and kept them. Some were inspired by our conversations and have brought me deeper insights on dimensions of leadership. I am delighted that they have now been collected together, so that others can share from Sarah's research and insights and benefit from her leadership experience working with executives.

Pieter Engelbrecht, Chief Executive Officer, Shoprite Holdings

An enticing flip side to Sarah's first book which was a 'how to' guide. This collection provides seeds for the curious leader; a multiple starter packet of thought leadership and inspiration in neat short form, easy to digest, useful to slingshot your thoughts forwards. When as a leader you feel an issue gnawing at you - there will be a matching insight to start you journey from right here - keep this book close at hand

Andrew Woodburn, Managing Director,
Woodburn Mann Executive Search

A quality which continues to set a true master of their art apart from their peers is their ability to take their audience through the journey of the most intricate concepts without losing them for one single step of the way.

Combine the above with a passion for leadership and conscious living, deeply rooted at the essence of her being and you have the delight of Sarah's presence. With the collaboration of these thought pieces, Sarah yet again guides each of us on our journey, putting some of the toughest leadership principles within the grasp of each of us. Making theory a practical reality that will continue to change our world.

Christo Els, Chief People Officer, Mentis

Sarah's blogs for CEOs are practical, inspirational, well written and personal – you can hear Sarah's voice coming through the pages as you read them.

Sarah's insights both guide and affirm issues experienced by leaders on their journey. This is a book that you would want to go back to time and again.

Christo Els, Senior Partner, Webber Wentzel

I have really come to enjoy Sarah's blogs and often read them over and over as I reflect on my role as a leader. The various dimensions of leadership are complex and leading in today's time requires a competence that cannot quite be learnt in a classroom and that is knowing what to do when you don't know what to do. As leaders we often find ourselves in those situations. Sarah always reminds me that learning agility and resilience are two essential ingredients of good leaders. She has the uncanny ability to take complex leadership challenges that are shared with her and simplify it in her blogs in a way that resonates with me at a deep level. I reflect on her blogs in my journey as a leader and it has become essential tools in my toolkit as I navigate the volatile roads now and the ones that lie ahead. As William Shakespeare put it "Brevity is the soul of wit". Sarah's blogs are witty, concise and profound. A must read for sure and a treasure to have on your bedside table.

Lee-Ann Samuel, Group Executive: People
Impala Platinum Holdings Limited

In this book Sarah Arnot has charted a course for making the most of the opportunities you have as a leader.

It's filled with valuable stories and lessons on taking control, becoming the best leader you possibly could be and how to create a winning culture in your organisation.

Hal Luscombe, Former Wales Rugby Player,
Business Owner (Luscombe+CO), Investor and Author

The metaphor in the introduction, to "move the dial on leadership", reminds me of the intricate parts and mechanics of a superior watch. In my mind this is analogous to the nature of human leaders who have a complex mix of features: emotion, intelligence, experience, culture, and habits. This intricacy of human mechanics makes it tough for an executive coach to shift a leader's thinking: to move his dial. Despite this, Sarah's stories prove she is shaping breakthroughs in leadership thinking; she is creating superior leaders. Her CEO blogs are compelling, easy to read, and insightful for everyone. A book to be read and shared.

Caroline Dale, Founder, The Thesis Coach

First published in 2020.

ISBN: 978-1-86922-868-2 (Printed)
eISBN: 978-1-86922-869-9 (PDF eBook)

Published by KR Publishing
P O Box 3954
Randburg
2125

Republic of South Africa

Tel: (011) 706-6009
Fax: (011) 706-1127
E-mail: orders@knowres.co.za
Website: www.kr.co.za

Typesetting, layout and design: Cia Joubert, cia@knowres.co.za
Cover design: Marlene De Lorme, marlene@knowres.co.za
Proofreading: Valda Strauss: valda@global.co.za
Project management: Cia Joubert, cia@knowres.co.za

KEEP YOUR FOCUS

40 Thought-Pieces on Maintaining Your Top Performance

SARAH ARNOT MULHERN

kr
publishing

2020

For my clients and colleagues, past and present

TABLE OF CONTENTS

ACKNOWLEDGEMENTS

Writing a book is a team effort and I depend on the feedback and support of my friends, family and colleagues as early readers to offer comment and criticism. They don't hold back, they encourage and give feedback, and of course any errors are entirely mine.

Once again, Sophie Kevany has provided invaluable editing support. The editing process holds me to account. Sophie is never afraid to question my thinking, or the clarity of my voice when describing complex topics.

My MPhil workgroup or Triad have once again been wonderful. Caroline Dale, Deborah Williams and Victor Kotze, each of you knows how much you've done to help me since I first met you. As thinking partners, your brilliance always inspires.

These thought pieces come about because of the work that we do at the Woodburn Mann Leadership Science Institute which Andrew Woodburn and I founded in 2018. I am grateful to Andrew for his confidence in our venture from the day we met.

Simon Camerer introduced me to Andrew and he and his wife Christine Service are the most stalwart of fun friends.

A very special thank you to our team at the Woodburn Mann Leadership Science Institute and to the broader team at Woodburn Mann Executive Search, especially Clara Woodburn, Candice Silverstone, Shanya van Niekerk, and Claire Kedzierski, let's carry on having great fun and doing fantastic work for our clients.

Thanks to Yvonne Pennington who has provided a shoulder to cry on, a listening ear, and countless suppers accompanied by delicious wine. As well as much laughter and a deep knowledge of the African bush which I have learned to love ever more in her company, particularly at Mashatu Game Reserve where some of my best writing gets done.

Friends who support me in life's journey, who keep me ambitious and keen to compete both at work and in sport through my fifth decade of life, include (in no particular order) Henry Gwyn Jones, Niall Quirk and his husband Dorian Broadwater, Allan and Coo Taylor, Linda and Patrick Taylor, Colette de Vries and her partner Charles Back, Serena Prest and her family, Daniela Smit, Missy and George Morgan, Ciara and Richard Francis, Anna Roberts Antonsson, Liz Van Rensburg, Georgina Pennington, Julia Pennington, Tim Rudd, Francis Garrard, Stephen Ball, Paulette and Mike Doo among others. I love you all to bits, I certainly couldn't do it without you.

My stepchildren Christopher and Ola Arnot, Robyn and Alistair van Rooyen, and Lauren and Cameron Brown have been an amazing support through a tough year.

Thanks to my two brothers, Graham and Mark Mulhern and your families. You know what you mean to me. Thanks to Zita for being a great inspiration, support and Mum.

I am particularly blessed with wonderful clients who have become more than clients; they are friends who I deeply admire. We spend many hours together both in coaching and in planning leadership team assessment and development. Although my job is to be there for them as a sounding board and thinking partner I often think I should be paying them for the privilege because I learn so much from them. I am a different person because of the people I have had the honour to work with.

Much of our client work is confidential but with their permission I would particularly like to thank Pieter Engelbrecht, CEO of Shoprite, Lee-Ann Samuel, Group Executive, People of Implats, Alex Mhembere,

CEO of Zimplats, Christo Els, Senior Partner of Webber Wentzel, and Sally Hutton, Managing Partner of Webber Wentzel for their support over the past few years. I would also like to thank another Christo Els, who is Chief People Officer of Mentis. You are all the inspiration for these pieces, along with those clients who prefer not to be mentioned. Without you the book would not exist.

Finally, I want to thank my publisher, Wilhelm Crous of KR Publishing and his team, particularly Cia Joubert and Tina van der Westhuizen. When Wilhelm saw the manuscript of my first book *Find Your Focus: 5 Steps to Your Best Year Ever*, he immediately agreed to publish it and has been supportive and encouraging ever since. Thank you, Wilhelm, for your tenacity and your insights. This is a better book because of you.

ABOUT THE AUTHOR

Sarah Arnot Mulhern is Managing Partner of the Woodburn Mann Leadership Science Institute, which provides leadership development and assessment services to Boards, CEOs and senior executives in Southern African corporate businesses. The Woodburn Mann Leadership Science Institute brings the science of leadership to the boardrooms of Africa.

Sarah's career spans more than 25 years, most of it spent at two companies – Accenture and Spencer Stuart – based in Ireland, France, the UK and South Africa. She held international leadership roles in both organisations. As an executive search consultant at Spencer Stuart she led the European Internet Practice and the European Software Practice. After moving to South Africa, she joined the Leadership Advisory Services (LAS) practice, consulting to global clients in multiple industries.

Sarah gives motivational talks based on her experience in sport and business and offers expert leadership advice on television and radio.

Sarah is also an amateur three-day eventer, which is a three-phase Olympic equestrian sport that includes dressage, show jumping and cross country. She has held leadership roles in the sport, acting as President of Western Cape Eventing for nine years and sitting on the Board of Eventing SA.

Sarah holds BA (Hons) and MA degrees from Trinity College, Dublin and an MPhil (Executive Coaching) from the University of Stellenbosch Business School.

"We cannot lead others if we cannot lead ourselves and the hallmark of leadership is responsibility."

Thuli Madonsela
Professor of Law, Stellenbosch University
Former South African Public Protector

INTRODUCTION

Leadership, CEO coaching, and how this book came to be

In early 2018, my business partner Andrew Woodburn and I founded the Woodburn Mann Leadership Science Institute (WMLSI) to build a specialised set of executive assessment and development tools that consistently uses the latest thinking about learning, leadership, decision-making and growth to help executives "move the dial" on leadership.

Over the past few years, as I worked with clients on assessing and developing executive leaders, and completed an MPhil in executive coaching and leadership, I realised that our knowledge about leadership and decision making comes principally from four academic disciplines: leadership theory; behavioural economics; neuroscience; and psychology, both behavioural and positive. I will elaborate on these throughout this book.

Part of the MPhil journey was learning academic writing again, something I hadn't done since my undergraduate years. I enjoyed the formality of the research and the robust quality of conclusions derived from high-quality peer reviewed academic literature. All of our work at WMLSI is now based on this principle. I often illustrate my ideas with stories from my life or my work with clients, but the points are grounded in solid research. You will find some of the key sources at the back of this book.

Business has generally lagged in terms of taking up and really applying this thinking to leadership. The early adopters were sports teams and individual athletes. Sporting literature becomes ever more interesting as new research into the importance of health, nutrition, recovery and mindset is published. Our understanding of how to deliver peak performance grows all the time and much of this research can also be applied to leadership in business.

Similarly, some of the world's major military organisations also use this type of thinking to develop leadership. My stepson is a member of the Army Reserve and his leadership training uses the approaches I describe in this book. In a world of constant change, where the fight is against an unknowable enemy, often terrorist or guerrilla in nature, the military chain of command can no longer be hierarchical and simply based on "command and control". Instead, soldiers need to be able to operate in smaller, agile and empowered units. Survival comes from the ability to think for themselves and their unit and being able to take good decisions in the field in real time. This is the approach described by Jocko Willink and Leif Babin in their books that transcribe the learnings of the US Navy Seals in Iraq to business leadership[1].

At WMLSI we have developed a framework for leadership that is also derived from these disciplines, in combination with two interviewing techniques that have stood the test of time: competency interviewing and situational interviewing.

This blend of a solid research-based framework and well-tested interviewing techniques allows us to offer one of the world's most comprehensive leadership assessment and executive development programmes. It is designed for executive leaders who want to significantly improve their skills, their performance and, perhaps most importantly, their job satisfaction.

Keep Your Focus is a collection of my most useful leadership research findings, distilled into a series of briefings or "blogs" as I've called them. I first wrote these pieces for my CEO coaching clients, who are chronically short on reading and research time. In truth, everyone can benefit from the insights they offer.

---

1   See Blog on "Extreme Ownership", page 66.

You might ask, and it's a good question, how does one become a CEO coach? As a proponent of planning one's life success, I am almost embarrassed to admit that it came about entirely by accident.

One day in early 2015 I received a call from a COO whom I had recently assessed as a finalist candidate for a big CEO role in South Africa.

"Sarah, I enjoyed our engagement and I appreciated the feedback you gave me when we ast talked. I'd like to work with you on developing some of the areas you suggested. Would you have time to do that? My ambition is to be CEO of my company."

I was working at Spencer Stuart, one of the world's leading executive search firms, and we had developed assessment tools that have become a global gold standard for this kind of work. This is no mere bank of psychometrics. Our assessment tools went far deeper and were personalised for every single participant in our programmes.

When Spencer Stuart's Johannesburg office was asked to find a CEO for a large, stock exchange listed South African company, they asked me to help. The name of the company is confidential but many of South Africa's top business leaders were involved, either as CEO candidates or as board members. Because the board needed to assess the potential risks and opportunities offered by each candidate we had to conduct deep dive assessments on each one. These types of assessments offer a much broader view than a typical executive search process and this approach is now global best practice for boards looking for CEO candidates internally and externally. At the time though, this kind of deep risk assessment for CEO candidates was new in South Africa.

One of the candidates was COO of a large South African business and another was a legendary corporate CEO. Both had opened up to me during their assessments and shared their world and the challenges they faced. After that search process was over I gave them some feedback on the outcome and when, a few weeks later, both called and asked me to coach them, I felt I could help, so I said yes.

I had an exclusive contract with Spencer Stuart and I asked if they would allow me to coach these two leaders. To my surprise the firm was fine with it. They trusted me to develop good relationships that would be to their benefit. That was it. With neither credentials, nor experience in this space, I was a CEO coach. That COO did become CEO not long afterwards. I take no credit for that; the work is always done by the client, not the coach, but I hope I may have been a catalyst for his confidence and some good thinking on dimensions of leadership that would serve him on his journey.

Although this opportunity came up unexpectedly, I had been thinking about the possibility of CEO coaching for a while. When one of my ex-colleagues, Jason Chaffer, left Spencer Stuart he joined Manchester Square Partners in London to focus on CEO coaching and he'd been kind enough to share his business model. I knew CEO coaching was an avenue potentially available to me.

I quickly realised that one should not coach without proper credentials. Being of an academic bent, I signed up for an MPhil in Leadership and Coaching at the University of Stellenbosch Business School, just 40 minutes from home. I left Spencer Stuart too, after 16 wonderful years with the firm. The global travel was becoming too much and I hankered after a different, more South African life. Though the following years would prove to be tough, as my Euro-based income evaporated, this was the best possible decision I could ever have taken.

I've written about the challenges of study and thesis writing in my first book, *Find your Focus*, so I won't repeat it here. The MPhil was a wonderful journey, hard work and humbling. I learned the value of reflection, the power of meditation, the importance of academic research, and made some lifelong friends. As I studied, I continued working, both on assessment assignments for other well-known headhunting firms and coaching clients of my own, including CEOs.

That combination of coaching leaders while studying was a perfect route to better understanding the gap that often exists between academic ideals and the day to day reality of being a leader.

Not only are CEOs short on time to read, their energies are consumed in so many ways that even space to think is often in short supply. That's where true leadership comes in. Let me elaborate on this, because it's a vital part of what I do and why I do it.

When you are CEO of a large business you have to follow evolving global situations as well as deal with social partners like government, unions and regulatory bodies. You need to understand the competition and the market, and you need to develop short- and long-term strategies. Handling a broad range of stakeholders is another absolute necessity. You must engage with politicians, the analysts and the media. Everyone wants a piece of you. You need to do all of this while taking hundreds of decisions, all the time, with imperfect data. The CEO really matters. That's why their remuneration looks out of sync with everyone else's. Ultimately, they drive it all, like the president of a nation. Not only does the buck stop with them, but everything depends on them and their style. Their influence is easy to underestimate, so let's look at some different examples: US Presidents.

Perhaps we won't look to President Donald Trump. He's not someone I would suggest role modelling as a leader. President John F Kennedy might be better. He had his detractors and his weaknesses but he left an indelible mark on the world. When he was assassinated on that terrible day in Dallas there was so much left for him to do but already he had set man on course to the moon and resolved the Cuban Missile Crisis. He was ahead of his time, a master politician, unbelievably courageous. He said:

Let us not be blind to our differences -- but let us also direct attention to our common interests and to the means by which those differences can be resolved.

In modern terminology, that's a fine definition of social intelligence[2]; recognising that others are different and seeking to find common ground. Bear in mind that in this speech he was talking about the US relationship with Russia at a tense moment in their relationship.

As a leader, Kennedy imbued the nation with hope. His youthfulness and energy were in keeping with the times. The world loved America then, and was devasted when he was assassinated after only a thousand days in office. He symbolised all that the nation wanted to be. He sided with the disabled and with minorities. He may not have been perfect in his personal life but his moral judgement on the important political issues of his time was bold and impressive.

What about President Ronald Reagan? His legacy is mixed. Some see him as one of the greatest presidents. Others can never forgive his part in the HIV/AIDS crisis of the 1980s when Reagan's refusal to address the epidemic, because he saw it as a "queers' disease", cost so many lives over the years. Yet, two positive things in his presidential style stand out. He is famous for having surrounded himself with great people, much smarter than he was and he fully acknowledged this. He said:

Surround yourself with the best people you can find, delegate authority, and don't interfere as long as the policy you've decided upon is being carried out.

That is one of the clearest stamps of great leadership.

---

2   See Part 2 on Social Intelligence.

Reagan also led one of the most remarkable financial transformations of the US economy, much as Prime Minister Margaret Thatcher did in the UK. There is a view that suggests he began the inexorable process of moving American wealth from the middle classes to the wealthy; if true, I would argue it was an unintended consequence of the decisions he took then.

He also understood something Western capitalist economies are at risk of forgetting – the danger of inflation – when he said:

> *Inflation is as violent as a mugger, as frightening as an armed robber and as deadly as a hit man.*

We would do well to remember that as we move into a post-coronavirus world.

There are many examples to draw from Reagan's long presidency, good and bad. The end of the Cold War, the fall of the Berlin Wall, the Iran-Contra scandal and much more. The point is that America at that time was absolutely defined by the man at the top, as Britain was by Thatcher. Strong leaders can achieve extraordinary things and whether you like what they achieved or not, both Thatcher and Reagan left an indelible stamp on the 1980s.

Thus it is with CEOs. Companies are defined by the person who runs the business. No job in the company is more important. The tone is set at the top. The CEO doesn't have to be the most brilliant person in the company. They don't have to take all the big decisions, indeed they shouldn't. Like a leading politician, the CEO of a big company needs to be able to recruit a great team, to fully delegate responsibility and authority, and then give themselves space to do "What only the CEO can do."[3]

---

3   See blog on "What only the CEO can do", page 89.

All of this makes coaching CEOs challenging, often intimidating, and unusually rewarding. I have thought deeply about the role I play in the lives of my clients. My conclusion is that much of my value lies in being a well-informed outsider and thinking partner. For some, I am quite literally the only person in their life who has no skin in their game. They can tell me anything; I will not judge or betray them. They owe me nothing beyond the monthly retainer. They can call me any time and I think about them all the time. The dynamic has resulted in the blogs pieces in this collection, all based on topics that my clients and I have pondered together.

I may sometimes feel unsure, but I am never afraid. While I respect my clients deeply, my position does not depend on their goodwill, unlike most of the people around them. The worst they can do is fire me. That's not going to change my life. I ask them to commit to six months work together. But if it is not working I don't hold them to it. Most work with me for at least six months, after which some feel they have got what they needed out of the coaching process. Others remain clients, on and off, for many years. In every encounter, I am honoured and enriched by the conversations we have and we touch on myriad subjects.

I fell into a habit early on of digging deeper into those topics and sending my client a summary of the findings. I called them blogs. The research was, and continues to be, time consuming and adds nothing to my pocket, but it adds greatly to my knowledge. It also became clear that many of these pieces were relevant to more than one client and I started sharing them more broadly.

As I was writing one particular piece, "The Cloak of Power"[4], I realised it might at some point become more than just a series of blogs. "The Cloak of Power" is a whimsical, research-based piece: an allegory, with a touch of the mythical. I shared it more widely and everyone liked it.

---

4   See blog on "The Cloak of Power", page 21.

It eventually went to my publisher with a note from me saying: "I'm imagining a small book, piled high on the counter at Exclusive Books. You might buy it to read on the plane, to keep in your loo, or on your desk as a reference. Something to dip into when you need inspiration or to be reminded of what's important as a leader. Wilhelm replied "I really like these. Let's do the book."

The result is in your hands: *Keep Your Focus*. I have loved researching and writing these pieces and I hope you will find them useful.

Part 1

MINDSET

FEAR AND COURAGE

Fear

Several recent interactions I've had with senior executives in large public companies in South Africa and around the world have highlighted a legacy culture of fear in their organisations. A good indicator of that fear is the number of talented individuals, operating two or three levels below the CEO, who are unwilling to promote their ideas, or to engage and innovate beyond their direct remit. Staying inside the box is safe. Anything else could result in disaster for the employee. In South Africa we often see these problems as specific to us. However, my experience is that this is a challenge for large organisations globally and one that can only be addressed by direct action from the CEO and Human Resources.

Ironically the organisations of which I am thinking all have CEOs with whom I have worked closely, who I greatly admire, and who themselves operate with notable courage. In many cases they have succeeded CEOs with a strong authoritarian management style.

Despite the leadership and role-modelling provided by these new CEOs the legacy of fear has not left their organisations. Years after a dominant and authoritarian leader leaves a business, the culture of fear they entrenched may continue to drive the behaviour of executives and managers.

The role of the CEO and her HR team is to change this. Innovation and creativity suffer in a culture of fear. The inability to question your hierarchical superior can result in disaster. The ultimate example of this was the Korean Airline plane crashes described by Malcolm Gladwell in *Outliers: The story of success*. In studying the high incidence of crashes, researchers found that the root cause was that co-pilots would never question the action of the captain, even if it was clearly wrong, and this would lead to the plane crashing and the death of everyone on board. Changing this culture was hard, but essential.

The hierarchical "command and control" culture highlighted by the Korean Airline crash is rooted in army structures, developed over many centuries, because a rigid chain of command and absolute discipline was necessary to fight the structured battles and traditional wars of the past. That has changed in a volatile, uncertain, complex, and ambiguous (VUCA) world, where guerrilla warfare and terrorism mean soldiers need to be able to take decisions in real time. Authority has been devolved to the smallest possible fighting units. As Justin Maciejewski, a former brigadier in the British Army, puts it:

I've been really shocked by how much fear is used as a motivator in business – in a way that I never saw it used as a motivator in the army. People are very much in a state of fear, not because they're being shot at, but because there's an internal fear working in terms of how people are being evaluated and watched all the time.

This culture of fear derives from an old-fashioned vision of leadership and power. CEOs need to be wary of the incremental impact of power and to avoid its negative impacts. Bob Iger, CEO of Disney, says that it's all too easy to get used to everyone waiting to hear where the CEO stands before they express their view, bring you new ideas, or even disagree. You need to work consciously and actively to fend off the corrosive effect of long-term power, to encourage debate and even dissent. This is true as much for CEOs as for leaders in other powerful positions, who may mirror behaviours they have long seen in those they report to.

Organisational fear has an impact on culture and ultimately success. Its presence is evidenced by behaviours in the business. If your people are fearful of sharing bad news, particularly if they have made a mistake, that is one sign. If they are reluctant to disagree with you publicly, that is another. If your team lacks diversity, you may find you are subject to groupthink, which is conducive to both a lack of innovation and a culture of fear. A key indicator is how people respond to feedback. Tough feedback can be hard to take and good leaders take it well and act on it. Bad leaders are combative and may be resentful when given tough feedback.

Fear-based cultures can be actively toxic. If bad behaviours in leadership are not addressed people will hide, cover up and do what they need to do to survive, not to thrive. Toxic behaviour can escalate and, if it is tolerated, will inspire more bad behaviour because it is seen as the best way to progress. Ultimately, this can destroy an organisation's public image. There are examples of this in the management culture at both Uber and Wells Fargo.

At Uber the former CEO, Travis Kalanick, was widely considered to have created an aggressive and dysfunctional culture. This led to claims that complaints about sexual harassment and racial discrimination were being ignored and this eventually lead to the departure of both the CEO and the Head of HR. Even the company's IPO filing was forthright about the risks embodied by its culture of hustle, business at all costs and the issues caused by lack of transparency in the internal culture.

At Wells Fargo fear drove bankers to create thousands of fraudulent customer accounts and assign them PINs (a process known internally as "pinning") so that they could charge customers for products they had not bought and didn't even know they had.

How do you address bad behaviour and ultimately break down the culture of fear?

- Confront bad behaviour visibly and directly

- Base bonuses on performance and behaviour, not performance alone

- Do not tolerate emoticnal "explosions" at any level, encourage a culture of respect

- Encourage two-way communication

- Encourage people to speak up, especially with dissenting ideas (see Blog on "Decisions and Judgement" for ideas on how to do this)

- Clearly define values and adhere to expectations around behaviour

- Finally, encourage a culture where "mistakes" are seen as learning opportunities to be quickly, and supportively, uncovered and shared

Courage

> *It is not the critic who counts; not the man who points out how the strong man stumbles, or where the doer of deeds could have done them better. The credit belongs to the man who is actually in the arena, whose face is marred by dust and sweat and blood; who strives valiantly; who errs, who comes short again and again, because there is no effort without error and shortcoming; but who does actually strive to do the deeds; who knows great enthusiasms, the great devotions; who spends himself in a worthy cause; who at the best knows in the end the triumph of high achievement, and who at the worst, if he fails, at least fails while daring greatly, so that his place shall never be with those cold and timid souls who neither know victory nor defeat.[5]*

What gives a man, or a woman, the courage to step into the arena, aware of the risks and the consequences, yet to step in regardless? Courage comes not from the absence of fear, but from facing that fear, being fully aware of all the possible adverse consequences. Courage requires self-confidence, vulnerability, the ability to back yourself and to step up to the challenge, despite the risks.

The CEOs I work with all have immense courage. Yet I do not always see that same courage reflected deeper in their organisations. Why not? What is it about business structures that depletes courage?

Leaders like to think they empower their staff; that they are free to say whatever they want. More often those very employees don't say what they think at all; indeed they are afraid of the consequences of saying what they think. Speaking up often takes courage and considerable self-confidence. A culture of fear will erode self-confidence fast, so if you see the symptoms in your organisation, that is the first thing you need to address.

---

5   From the speech *"Citizenship in a Republic"*. Theodore Roosevelt, 1910

Responsibility for confident and courageous behaviour lies on both sides of the fence: with the leader and also with the employee. Creating a forum where all ideas are welcome, and any issue can be raised without consequence, no matter how tough, is one way to uncover how your employees really co feel.

Encourage employees to take risks and to act with courage. This means addressing behaviour throughout the management team so that they listen uncritically to input and feedback. This is hard. But if you encourage that listening, and at the same time, encourage employees to have confidence, perhaps starting with small things, it gets easier for everyone. The result will be a more vibrant, open, and innovative culture.

Fear of failure

During the Coronavirus lockdown I was asked to contribute to a series of webinars for the South African equestrian community. My topic was leadership in equestrian coaching and the question came up: "How do you handle fear of failure? What if that gets in your way?" When we are assessing senior executives, we sometimes pick up fear of failure as a major limitation to them realising their full potential. Fear of failure is one of the most significant and challenging barriers to success.

Causes of fear of failure

Why is fear of failure so debilitating and why does it run so deep that even the most successful people can find themselves hampered by it?

Some answers can be found in neuroscience and behavioural economics. Humans have evolved to have a freeze, fight or flight mechanism. We react violently to the bad things that happen to us, to the extent that we apply fear to harmless situations. If we've been affected by PTSD or other anxiety disorders, fear can become completely paralysing.

Another human characteristic is loss aversion, as described by Daniel Kahneman in *Thinking Fast and Slow*. Once we possess something, we are extremely averse to losing it, even if it was something we didn't particularly care about in the first place. Being unable to try something new can be rooted in the fear that we might lose what we already have.

Perfectionists are often paralysed by fear, which leads to procrastination. Procrastination can be the voice that says that doing something may be worse than doing nothing.

What can we do about fear of failure?

One of the best techniques s to redefine failure into learning opportunities. I love to do this. When I started my new business, I was frustrated by the number of business development calls that didn't translate into new business. I talked to my partner about it and we sat down and looked at the numbers. We realised that about one in four proposals was being accepted, which actually seemed like a good hit rate for a completely new business. Even better, that discussion about failure pointed to a new growth strategy: focus on setting up more new client business meetings and getting them to the point of asking for a proposal.

> *Failure is just the price we pay for success.*
> John Maxwell, *Failing Forward, 2000*

The same applies to job-hunting. Sending out endless applications that result in a "no" or worse still, complete silence, can feel like a demoralising failure. Going through interviews and not being offered the job feels the same. If you look at it differently: all the "no's" in the world serve you on the journey to "yes!"

Use the experience of all those rejections positively to adapt and refine your job search process. Spend your time researching job seeking strategies that work and applying those to your own search. Pivot the failures; turn them into learning.

As Robert Kiyosaki, author of *Rich Dad Poor Dad* and many other great books on personal finance says, "In my own life, I've noticed that winning usually follows losing."

This is also true in sport and the performing arts. I was watching a friend of mine give her little daughter a riding lesson the other day. Little Alice had fallen off her pony when she was learning to canter and now she was nervous. Learning to canter is a scary thing because you have to push the horse, or in this case pony, to go faster, to a point where you feel out of control. It's like learning to downhill ski – there's a moment when you have to embrace the loss of control in order to improve and enjoy it more. Facing down that fear is part of the exhilaration.

Alice did just that. There were some tears and some "I don't want to" moments that broke her Mum's heart and made her want to stop pushing her child. But Mum is a very good rider and she knew that the joy comes from breaking through those moments of fear and realising the joy of greater speed and a different caliber of stride beneath you. That day Alice got it. A day later her Mum had to stop her from doing nothing but canter. Because she loved it so much. What a difference a day can make.

Thomas Edison believed, "Many of life's failures are people who did not realise how close they were to success when they gave up."

Most of us have a child like Alice buried deep inside us. Even those who we think of as brave and successful. There's an inner voice in most of us that says, "What if it goes wrong?", "What if I make a fool of myself?" "What if they don't like me?" "What if I get hurt?" That voice makes us feel uncomfortable and stressed. It paralyses us.

Success, satisfaction, exhilaration and even joy lie beyond those feelings. There are some techniques you can use to help yourself face down the fears and move forward. I like Tim Ferris in his Tedtalk "Why you should define your fears." It's a short one, well worth watching. Essentially, it's about facing your fears head on by writing them down. Then thinking how bad it will be if it comes true and what you can do to mitigate that. Finally, what is the cost of not doing the thing you fear?

South African general Jan Smuts declared, "A man is not defeated by his opponents but by himself."

If any of this resonates with you, then put the effort into learning to think differently about failure, see it as no more than your opportunity to learn and to pivot to the next great thing in your life.

Vulnerability

I write two blogs – one on the fynbos (indigenous plant life) that grows on our farm[6] and a private blog for my CEO clients on topics of leadership and life.

Never have the two crossed – indeed I paused The Fynbos Blog in early 2019 after six years of sharing the stories and photos of the plants I saw while out running with my dogs, the adventures we had and the flowers we discovered.

I was recovering from a bout of pneumonia and my housekeeper, Louise, bought a lovely arrangement of wild-flowers into my room. To my astonishment one of them was *Lucospermum lineare*, a protea known as "The Vulnerable". This rare plant is on "the red list" and close to extinction. There were a few on our farm but they were wiped out by fires in early 2017 (see The Story of the Fire on the Fynbos Blog) and I was afraid we had lost them forever. Yet here it was, a delicate lovely flower giving me succour as I dosed through days of fever and recovery.

Finally, on a clear, still day, when I was feeling much better, I walked out with the dogs in search of this rare beauty. I found many of them, growing on the slope above the driveway, higher up than they used to be which is why I hadn't seen them from the road. As I walked, I pondered its common name: "The Vulnerable".

I am a fan of Brene Brown, whose academic work on vulnerability and shame has helped me to understand my own lack of confidence and why so many of my brilliant clients suffer from the same feelings, despite being outwardly confident and successful.

We cannot succeed if we are not prepared to expose ourselves to criticism. Fear of exposure, fear of failure are human characteristics,

---

6   The Fynbos Blog, www.fynbosblog.com

even for those most outwardly bold and brave. Understanding this connection helps to create true confidence. A confidence linked to humility and an acceptance of our own vulnerability. Fire brought successful propagation and regrowth to our rare, delicate *Lucospermum lineare*. Exposing ourselves to the fire of public criticism, whether in sport or in business is the only way to succeed, learn and grow. Fire and criticism are both terrifying, yet once through the flames we build confidence and grow stronger. Every time.

Figure 1: Lucospermum Lineare "The Vulnerable"

Setting Intentions

We are all subject to confirmation bias: we tend to see the world as we expect to see it, and unconsciously seek confirmation of our expectations. If you've got a colleague who you perceive to be "difficult", you'll be looking for evidence of that, and it's very likely you will find plenty of it.

Confirmation bias isn't all bad – it's part of "thinking fast": the automatic processes of our brains that allow us to navigate the world without having to second guess every single decision. Without these "fast" thought processes we wouldn't be able to operate efficiently. They enable us to automate many of the things that we do, whether it's driving a car, playing tennis, or swiftly picking out the salient points from a spreadsheet full of data, simply because we quickly recognise "normal", making anything abnormal jump out. This particular mind-model comes from Daniel Kahneman, the Nobel prize-winning psychologist who lays out 40 years of research in his seminal book *Thinking Fast and Slow*.

Confirmation bias is just one of these filters. There are many others and to learn more about them I highly recommend Kahnemans's book. For our purposes, the trouble with these filters is that sometimes they impact our behaviour in ways we don't appreciate, and when you are the boss, your behaviour influences the behaviour of those around you. The good news is that we can take charge of this ability to filter the world, turn it around, and use it positively to enhance our ability to handle our work and life.

I combine two techniques to do this to best effect. One is called "6 things" which I explained in detail in my book *Find Your Focus: 5 steps to your best year ever*. The other is setting intentions.

"6 Things": Think about what you need to get done today. Write them down.

Writing down our **real** priorities for each day helps us stay focussed. Some people like to do this the night before. It's not so much a to-do list, as reminders of the key things that need to be done. The best way is to keep it to no more than six items. There are lots of things you have to do, but what's really important? Commit to ticking those things off your list every single day. As well as getting the important stuff done, this golden-oldie will help improve your productivity and increase your sense of control.

Now set your intentions and focus on the outcomes.

What's the best way to achieve those daily goals? Imagine you need to have a difficult conversation with a colleague about their behaviour in board meetings. Keeping your desired outcomes in mind will help you stick to the business at hand and help you avoid triggering their defensive response. Or, or if they do become defensive, it should help you avoid becoming defensive in turn. The great advantage of focussing on the outcome is that you'll worry less about how you get there. It helps too if you attribute others with generally good intentions. That means you might find it easier to be more tolerant and put their negative behaviour down to them simply having a bad day, for example, rather than being side-tracked by it. The other plus is that it allows for the discussion to pick up on any positive content they offer.

Kahneman suggests that we are too judgemental in attributing behaviour to personality. Often behaviour is triggered by circumstances, which is why wonderful people may do stupid things and difficult people can sometimes show up as extremely kind.

In this example, it might be worth asking your colleague how *they* think board meetings could work better. Keep asking questions like "what else?" Really listen to what they have to say, not the tone they say it in. When you hear something that comes close to the topic you wanted to discuss, e.g. *their* poor behaviour, encourage them: "Yes, I agree it would be great if we all did this." Frame it positively, even if they framed it negatively. Asking questions helps you to stay in exploratory mode and avoids triggering any defensive responses (fight, flight, freeze) on either side. It means less emphasis too on the person's tone or personality. Another advantage is that by asking questions you are encouraging them to think more deeply on the topic. By listening really deeply to their comments, you are less likely to trigger their defensive mode.

In summary, think about the priority outcomes you want to achieve in a day or conversation. Check what assumptions might be driving your own behaviour, such as confirmation bias. If you can set good filters for your own behaviour by focusing on the outcomes you want, you'll find it easier to navigate difficult conversations because it will be easier to stay in exploratory mode.

Finally, if you find yourself becoming irritated, think "red head vs blue head" to see if you can move back to "exploratory" mode[7]. We will find out more about red and blue heads later on, but, for now, you can think of red head as the emotional state of mind and blue head as the calm state of mind. Then add the switch so you can flip between them.

---

7   See blog on "Self Management according to the All Blacks", page 30.

Imposter Syndrome

There is a strange thing that I hear from clients, CEOs and other C-suite executives in large corporates, most of whom are quite brilliant at what they do. They tell me they feel unworthy, that they are not really up to the job, not as good as others think they are. There's a name for this phenomenon – it's called "Imposter Syndrome" – and after two recent conversations about it during coaching sessions, I decided it was time to dig more deeply into this topic.

Men versus women

Imposter syndrome is reportedly more common in women than in men. Because of this, researchers have focused extensively on women and particularly women from minorities working in a range of fields from corporate business to the healthcare and academic sectors.

I suspect this is not true. My experience, though purely anecdotal, is that men may suffer every bit as much as women, but they are less willing to talk about it. In a trusted coaching relationship, they do raise the topic and I would suggest that 50% or more of the very senior people that I coach, both male and female, struggle with aspects of Imposter Syndrome.

I am almost embarrassed to admit here that I suffer from imposter syndrome myself. I work incredibly hard, all the time, to deepen my knowledge on the many aspects of leadership, just to feel that I have a right to share the room with the brilliant people who are my clients. That is why, when they tell me they have feelings of inadequacy, I completely understand.

Intelligent people versus stupid people

The people of the earth are divided by intelligence: no matter what gender, nationality, religion or race, most of us are not very clever, some of us are quite clever and a few are extremely clever. The distribution of global IQ fits on a standard bell curve, with about 2% scoring above 130 and 2.5% below 70 on intelligence tests.

One of the most interesting things about Imposter Syndrome is that it seems only to affect clever and extremely clever people. Less intelligent people do not seem to struggle with it at all. Albert Einstein suffered from it towards the end of his life. Shortly before he died, he said:

> The exaggerated esteem in which my lifework is held makes me very ill at ease. I feel compelled to think of myself as an involuntary swindler.

Neuroscientists suggest the reason for this is that less intelligent people are less likely to question their own thinking or accept that they are wrong. "They misunderestimated me," said George W Bush on a visit to Bentonville in Arkansas in 2000. Intelligent people are less likely to come to a definite point of view on matters, because they can see them from multiple points of view.

Clever and very clever people understand just how much there is to know about any topic and how limited their perspective is likely to be. When they have to make decisions in that uncertainty, as CEOs and senior executives do every single day, it's an exposure to risk because they cannot, or do not have time, to understand all the data. When they get it right, it might feel like luck got them there, rather than talent combined with experience.

Humility, curiosity and creativity

There are some benefits to Imposter Syndrome. For one thing it keeps us humble and humility is one of the greatest qualities of leadership, one that is incredibly easy to lose once inside the ivory tower of the boardroom or CEO's office.

Feelings of insecurity also drive curiosity, which makes us seek deeper understanding and more knowledge which, in turn, probably leads to better decision making. More knowledge gives you more ways to "join the dots" and think innovatively.

People like leaders who present as strong and decisive, even if they are stupid. We certainly see that in the world of politics. Good leaders with high intelligence have to balance their desire to question and understand deeply, with the need to take decisions quickly and with certainty. There is a paradox at the heart of this. One of the quirks of human behaviour is that we are drawn at times to leaders who are stupid because their very stupidity makes them appear strong and decisive.

Self-belief – thinking about others, not yourself

I am not sure that Imposter Syndrome goes away easily. If even Einstein developed it late in life, I suspect it may become more entrenched as we age, not less. However, if we can take it as a blessing, and see it as a signifier of intelligence, one that brings the benefits of humility, innovation and insecurity, all of which drive us to work harder, we might feel better about having it.

One of the best ways to know if you have it under control is if you are thinking about others, not yourself. If you are being overly insecure, you will probably tend to worry more about what others are thinking about you and that's not healthy or useful. If you can switch to thinking "How can I help others be successful?" you may find you can tone down the voice that tells you are not good enough.

Tony Blair Syndrome

Tony Blair had a great belief in his moral judgement. He stood outside No. 10 Downing Street, the British Prime Minister's residence, in 2003 and announced that the country would go to war because he believed that the evidence from the Joint Intelligence Group's dossier showed that Iraq had weapons of mass destruction. No evidence of such weapons was ever found and the effects of that war linger on today. Blair said, as he made his announcement, "Trust me, I'm a moral man." He believed it too. His wife is a practising Roman Catholic and his children went to Catholic schools. He himself later converted to Catholicism. His faith in his own superior moral judgement meant he genuinely believed he was right when he uttered those words. Both the belief in himself and the dossier turned out to be flawed.

Over many years of assessing successful executive leaders I began to notice that the most highly intelligent often face a similar challenge in judgement. I first picked it up when I was working in Paris. Executives who had attended the great and very selective French engineering school, *Polytechnique*, often had an unshakeable belief in the power of their own minds. This meant they could be quite destabilised and upset when they realised they hadn't performed as well as they expected to in an assessment.

In exactly the same way that Blair placed too much faith in the quality of his superior morality, they placed too much faith in their intelligence. Often, their brain delivers great solutions. They know that their ability to "join the dots" is faster and better than most others. They come to rely on that fantastic brain to give them the answer quickly, and sometimes they forget to listen to input from others.

There are good reasons not to trust your superior intellect or moral beliefs. Behavioural economics tells us that we are all subject to bias. Rapid, "join the dots" thinking is "fast thinking", and it is completely rooted in our biases and personal perspective. Listening openly to different views from other people can help us broaden our thinking and widen our perspective. Or, to put it another way: no matter how clever you are, you are unlikely to come up with the best possible answers to big, complex questions all by yourself.

Although we often have to take fast decisions and move quickly in business, we also need to pay attention when it comes to the bigger questions. Why? Because our first idea is rarely our best idea. Most often improvements come from tossing them around for a while, and getting input from "credible others".

What do I mean by "credible others"? One of the greatest investors in the world is Ray Dalio, who has written about his success in *Principles*. Dalio, an exceptionally intelligent man, points out that people offer ideas, views and opinions all the time, about everything. We should think of this as merely noise and pay attention instead to the views of a few "credible others". Thinking in terms of credible others can help us make better choices about who we work with to build better strategies and take better decisions.

The Cloak of Power

Eighteen months ago a friend of mine was promoted. He'd been in a senior position for years but found himself suddenly catapulted to the top job: CEO. We were having a cup of coffee one Saturday morning and he said, "The great thing, Sarah, is that I haven't changed at all." I looked at him with some bemusement. "Yes, you have," I said. "No," he assured me, "I haven't." This assertion was followed by a story demonstrating exactly how approachable he still was to the ordinary people in his business and his life.

I didn't say much more but smiled internally and made a mental note to do some more detailed research. How was it possible that this highly intelligent man didn't understand the aura of power this job conferred on him? Nor how his success in the job had changed so much about him?

The Invisible Cloak

Power is like an invisible cloak. But unlike the traditional version, which makes the wearer invisible, the cloak of power is invisible to the wearer and impossible for everyone else to ignore. That's why my friend thinks he hasn't changed: it's because he can't see his cloak of power. The problem with the cloak of power is that people filter all your words and actions through it. That has many ramifications. One of them is that the wearer appears far more intimidating than they mean to be. The greater the power, the thicker the cloak and the more distorted their actions can appear to others, even when they seem quite straightforward to them.

Social Intelligence

One of the reasons social intelligence is such an important attribute of leadership is that leaders need to take responsibility not only for the intention they put behind their words, but also for how their words are received by others. Great leaders flex their style in ways that take into account how their message will be perceived by the group or individual they are talking to at any point in time. This doesn't mean they are inauthentic. On the contrary, it means they are open to the feelings and motivations of others and prepared to take responsibility not only for what they say, but also for how it lands. If they take into consideration the cloak of power, even if they can't see it, they increase their social intelligence. Humour always helps, no matter how great the position and thick the cloak. If you can keep a genuine sense of humour and some humility, it makes the cloak of power a little less daunting to others.

Part 2

SOCIAL INTELLIGENCE

Social Intelligence – Dimensions of Social Intelligence

This is a multi-part series of short blogs on some of the many facets of social intelligence.

A few weeks ago I was talking to the very senior and successful Chief Financial Officer (CFO) of a JSE top 40 company. The woman in question was undeniably bright and had risen to the very top of her profession, having spent time at a blue-chip auditing firm and a series of large companies. She had found time to have two children along the way and had the strength of character to divorce her wealthy but unpleasant husband. "I'd rather work hard for my own money," she said, "than live with a man I can't respect." I liked and admired her.

The occasion of our conversation was a feedback session. Her board had asked my firm to assess their CEO and top team as part of their CEO succession planning process. They had also asked us to help the executives with their own development as leaders and assess how well the senior team was functioning. I had assessed Mpho (not her real name) a few weeks earlier and now we were discussing her report.

The CFO in a large corporate needs two key skills. The first is the ability to "helicopter"; that is, to be able to fly high and see far. Then to plunge into highly specific financial details (IFRS 16 accounting practices or dealing with hyperinflation in Angola, for example) and quickly grasp what they mean for the company, now and in the future. Good CFOs are also the strategic right-hand partner to the CEO, and they are absolutely key in formulating and contributing to company strategy.

Mpho was unusually good at this helicoptering and we discussed at length how she could more effectively use this skill. Then we looked at how she needed to boost her social intelligence. Social intelligence is a critical success factor for senior executives and is broadly lacking in executive leadership around the world. Of the people I have assessed over 15 years, I would estimate that 25% have good social intelligence. However, more than 60% of them need to develop their social intelligence while 15% may have the rudiments of social intelligence but they still need to work on understanding and developing some facets.

What do we mean by social intelligence?

The term was coined by Daniel Goleman in his 2008 book of that name, though he builds on the work of Gardner, Wilber and others. Goleman describes the skills we need to engage better with others in all aspects of our lives, at work, at home, with friends and wider family and anyone else with whom we have ongoing social contact. Social intelligence is the area where I work the hardest, with executives and in my own development. On the plus side, because it is so neglected, social intelligence is one of the easiest leadership dimensions to improve. One of the best ways to improve social intelligence is to work with a coach, but if you apply your mind to it, you can make great progress on your own.

As people grow their careers through their 20s and 30s, they lay the technical foundations for their future. Being good at the core technical aspects of whatever job they are doing, whether it be engineering, sales, marketing, finance, HR or anything else, is what will win them promotions until they finally reach the gilded title "Executive". When they do, these skills suddenly become far less important than the ability to connect and work well with others. No longer do you just manage down, now you have to manage sideways, working with your peers, and upwards, influencing your boss in a positive way. Your responsibility lies beyond your department, particularly if you sit on the Executive Committee of the business. You also need to manage your stakeholders, both external *and* internal, which means mapping them out, considering their relative importance, and then understanding the quality of your relationship with them, and how to improve that.

What is social intelligence?

My friend and ex-colleague, Justin Menkes, coined the term "Executive Intelligence" in his brilliant book of that name. He doesn't actually use the term "social intelligence" in the book, however his description of social intelligence remains my favourite. The following is extracted from Justin's book:

- Recognise the conclusions that can and cannot be drawn from a particular exchange
- Recognise the likely underlying agendas and motivations of individuals and groups that are involved in a situation
- Anticipate the likely emotional reactions of individuals to actions or communications
- Accurately identify the core issues and perspectives that are central to a conflict
- Appropriately consider the probable effects and unintended consequences that may result from taking a particular course of action
- Recognise and balance the different needs of all relevant stakeholders

The reason I believe social intelligence can be so easily and usefully developed at the executive level is that the process is straightforward. It simply involves applying the already analytic executive mind to a new data set: people. Fundamental to developing the six skills Justin described above is understanding that people are different, they all have different motivations, and that they are all subject to different biases and assumptions. When I discuss social intelligence as a development opportunity with executives, I start by asking them to identify people in their world who handle complex interpersonal situations well. Finding role models whose skills you can observe and imitate is a great way to start.

This short series on social intelligence is intended to give you some insight into how we can dial up our social intelligence and use these skills effectively in the world of business. New learning from neuroscience and behavioural economics can help us, as can some of the insights garnered from academic research on executive coaching.

Social intelligence – self-awareness

Social intelligence starts with silence. Your silence. If you want to understand others, you need to hear what they have to say.

Self-awareness is another fundamental trait to develop for social intelligence. In order to give yourself the space to understand others and potentially to influence them, you must be able to control your own reactions to any given situation.

When my colleague, Clara Woodburn, works with an Executive Coaching client she almost always starts with self-awareness. She gives her clients "homework" and the initial homework is to observe how they handle difficult multi-personal situations and then report back. As with many other areas of life, the first step to change is accepting who we are now. Only then can we map out a path that leads to new behaviours.

Have you ever seen someone get defensive in a meeting, feeling that they are being attacked or misunderstood? Have you ever seen anyone get angry in a meeting and raise their voice at a colleague, or worse, a subordinate? Have you ever seen someone cry in a meeting when they have been publicly criticised? Have you ever tried to give another person feedback only to have them become resentful and angry with you, even though you meant well and intended the feedback to be helpful and constructive? Or have you ever been the person feeling resentful and angry? If so, you are completely normal. In fact, I suspect that most of us could develop in self-management, which is the first key to social intelligence.

A word here about authenticity. There is a view that being an authentic leader means acting in accordance with how you feel. In other words, without self-management. In fact, that is the opposite of authentic leadership, which is instead grounded in self-awareness. Authentic leadership means having an internal and carefully considered ethical framework and engaging consistently with others, at all levels, based on those ethics and values. Developing social intelligence is an essential component of authentic leadership and the first step is self-awareness.

Social intelligence – self- management

Our ability to make good decisions deteriorates under pressure and stress. The physiological impact of stress can take over the quality decision-making structures of the brain and can mean that we become more impulsive. Neuroscientists call this "amygdala hijack" after the part of the brain that houses our primitive emotions. In general, men will take high-risk decisions in these circumstances, while women tend towards lower risk. In both cases we fail to evaluate the full range of options and make the wisest move.

You will have seen this play out in meetings. When the stress heightens, the table thumping becomes more likely. People who have a more pleasing and belonging mindset may become timid and quiet in these circumstances. Those with more aggressive tendencies will dominate the decision making, rightly or wrongly.

There are a number of techniques you can use to address this behaviour and manage your reactions so that you take better decisions. I have drawn the first from mindset and psychological work done with the New Zealand Rugby Team, the All Blacks. In 2007 the team "choked" in the Rugby World Cup, despite having all the skills and track record to win. They slunk home and immediately became early adopters of one of the most powerful assets in sport: mindset.

While the team experimented with a variety of tools to enhance their mindset, one of my favourites, because it is so simple, is the concept of "red head/blue head". Red head and blue head are states of mind. Red head is loss of emotional control: angry; sad; scared; excited; passionate; unpredictable, or any combination of these. Blue head is calm and exploratory. When your state of mind is "blue head" you can take a step back and see the whole field of play and very quickly make a good decision. The technique is quite simple: when you feel yourself becoming emotional you acknowledge that you are going into a red head state and you mentally flip the switch to blue head. Taking a deep breath helps and you might add a physical cue, like putting your hands together. In neurology they say, "what fires together wires together". That's why repetition is so valuable – the more you repeat any process, physical or mental, the more automatically your brain can execute the process. Keep practising, and if you enlist both breathing and your chosen physical cues in mildly stressful situations, you will soon find that they become useful and available in much more stressful situations.

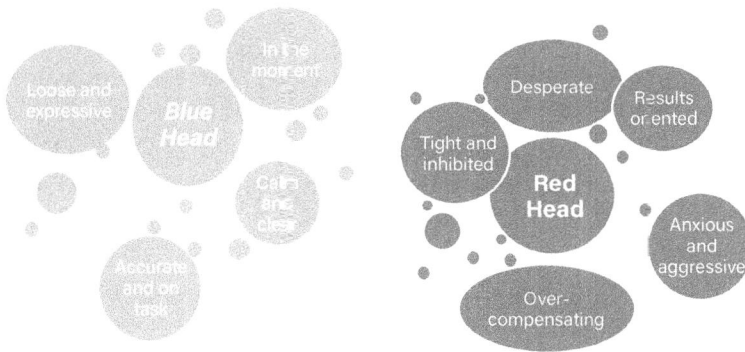

Figure 2: Managing your mind under pressure, using the blue head/red head technique

Self-distancing

When you discuss a friend's problem, it's incredibly easy to give advice on what they should do. Yet we are poor at doing this for ourselves. At the University of Michigan, they have a lab that studies emotion and self-control. Ethan Cross, who heads up the lab, has done numerous experiments on how self-distancing can help with taking your own advice.

Self-distancing employs another simple technique. When you are getting embroiled in a tough conversation, or when you feel yourself getting emotional, ask yourself: "How would I advise a friend who is in this situation?" I sometimes excuse myself from the room and go to a quiet place for a moment to reflect on this. When I come back to the discussion it is always with a calmer perspective and a wider range of options.

Social intelligence – choose your mentors

When my colleague, Candice Silverstone, and I carry out executive assessments, we inevitably notice that the stand-out trait of the best executives, the great leaders who get terrific 360 reviews from their bosses, peers and direct reports, is social intelligence. Of course, you have to be skilled at your job, which tends to be why you got promoted to the C-suite in the first place, but social intelligence is the path to greatness.

In many cases we also find that these leaders don't take social intelligence for grantec. They have invested in studying and understanding it as a critical skill to develop in their leadership journey.

The best way to develop social intelligence in the corporate world

Over the last 15 years of assessing "C" level executives, one of the saddest things has been meeting wonderful people who have not developed social intelligence by their early 50s. It always makes me think: "If only I had got hold of you 10 years ago..." This is not to suggest that older people cannot learn these skills – on the contrary one of the most encouraging findings of neuroscience is that our brains continue to be capable of learning throughout our lives. However, the opportunity cost of not developing social intelligence by your early 40s can never be recouped.

My move into CEO coaching, and my passion for including coaching in many executive development programmes was motivated by the desire to help people develop social intelligence. I know from my horse-riding career that the best coaches are not necessarily the great riders, but rather the ones who have had to dig deep to develop their understanding precisely because they are not naturally gifted. In the same way, I was very clunky at social intelligence in my early career and until my mid-30s. Then I had the great good luck to be mentored by some wonderfully skilled senior colleagues, who themselves had been mentored by the previous generation. Those were critical years in my career; I found everything became so much easier as I developed the traits of social intelligence.

Mentors

That point is critical – to enhance our social intelligence we should ideally have mentors who will act as sounding boards to help us navigate complex interpersonal situations and to give us tough but developmental feedback on our performance at meetings. Coaching can also be helpful, but it lacks the real-time exposure that a mentor should have.

To find a good mentor, look at those around you and identify the people who seem best able to handle difficult interpersonal situations. Those who set meetings up for success before the meeting ever happens. Those who can tune into the motivations of a complicated group of people, who can moderate their style according to the audience and the situation. If you can identify such a person, approach them and ask if they will be your mentor. Or, if they are a peer, ask them if they will be your buddy and sounding board.

When you have a difficult or complex interpersonal situation to manage, go to your mentor first and say, "I've got this situation, here's how I'm thinking of handling it." After you have explained, ask them, "What would you do?" If you do that consistently two wonderful things will happen. First, you will probably develop a deep and trusting relationship with the person who is mentoring you, because people like to help others achieve their potential, and your humility in seeking help is very likely to build trust quickly. Second, you will start to think more broadly about the options available to you, and, as you try out new behaviours in these tricky situations, you will steadily become more skilled. The earlier you do this in your career, the more proficient you will become.

We learn by observing and by practising new behaviours until they become habits. If you are an ambitious CEO, a manager with your eye on the C-suite, or anything in between, developing your social intelligence is the single most useful investment you can make.

Social intelligence – Don't underestimate the introverts

My colleague Candice and I were assessing an executive called John the other day. He was a quiet man, confident, but not charismatic or a talker. Likeable, but perhaps a tad dull. It took quite a while to get him to drop his guard and open up, and I thought we might not even get there. He was an introvert. Introverts are deceptive as leaders because they don't belong to the outgoing, noisy school of leadership. Their influence is quieter and can sometimes go unnoticed. But just because they don't engage with a "Hail fellow, well met!" style, does not mean they lack social intelligence. John has exceptional social intelligence. He understands what we call "good" politics: the need to invest upfront in winning buy-in for important decisions. He knows how to support people, allow them to make mistakes and have their backs. He is patient and invests in a coaching style. He's not a walkover though, he's tough on performance, but he's invested. Management by abandonment, something we see all too often, is not his style. His introverted nature has not stopped him from excelling. It might even have helped.

I first learned about the social intelligence of introverts when I was very young, long before the label "social intelligence" had been invented and it was a powerful lesson.

When I finished school in Ireland, I didn't feel ready to go to university. Indeed, I wasn't sure I wanted to. I went to Oxford instead, to spend a year learning secretarial skills, meeting extraordinary people like Boris Johnson and many others who have since made their imprint on the world. It was a happy year and I made some lifelong friends.

I then went to London and worked in the City for two years as a secretary in a bank before I came to my senses and returned to Dublin to study at Trinity College. Those two London years were more difficult.

I was unsophisticated, Irish and unprepared for the big city. It left me with a dislike of London which remained until I was lucky enough to move there as a head-hunter in my 30s and in a much better position to enjoy the opportunities it presented.

As a 19-year-old I was an "A-type" in the wrong body, with the wrong job. I was insecure about everything. Always a bit overweight, never pretty enough, alright at my job but not great, socially immature and sexually even more so. In short, I was needy and struggling to find the kind of friendships that have supported me through most of my life. I was living in a flat with three other girls, all of us very different and some nicer than others. Emma, my favourite of the three, moved out, and this little mouse – to my mind – called Isobel (not her real name) moved in. Isobel worked at a large shop called the General Trading Store and although she pulled her weight in the flat, she didn't have much of a social life and she said little to nothing. I dismssed her as completely uninteresting.

Then the other two girls got into some serious trouble involving drugs and the police. Their parents were involved too. It was a period of relentless drama. Isobel and I were left in a state of mild shock. At home, just the two of us one evening, we opened a bottle of wine and started talking. She knew everything. Everything I had been blind to about the others and to my astonishment, pretty much everything about me. She opened up and once we'd bonded, we remained good friends for the rest of my time in London.

The lesson I learned that night was that when people are not speaking, they are listening, observing and thinking. The rest of us are just waiting for the gaps in the conversation so that we can have our say. Many years later a boss of mine said, "You have two ears and one mouth. Use them in that proportion." That, and my experience with Isobel, started me down the road of learning to listen, and even more so, of appreciating the introverts around me. Understanding that their internal life is just as rich as my own and quite possibly richer. I also learned that introverts can be excellent students of the foibles of human nature and often have good solutions to the problems we all face, if we take the time to ask them. Charisma and charm have their place. But they can be outshone by the skills of the silent who listen and who think.

Part 3

DIVERSITY

A South African Story

In 1987 a boy called Sifiso was born near the town of Springs, south of Johannesburg, under the shadow of a huge platinum refinery. He came from a humble background, but not one of extreme poverty. His father was a policeman and other family members included schoolteachers and nurses – educated but not of the professional classes. Sifiso was an ambitious child and his parents encouraged him to study. They all saw education as the only way to escape poverty. The school Sifiso attended wasn't great; it didn't even have a proper maths teacher. He studied hard despite the disadvantages.

Sifiso saw that the people working in the refinery had money. He used to look at the huge structures and think to himself: "Imagine if I were to run that refinery one day."

In 1989 Pravin, a young South African Indian man, came from Pietermaritzburg to work at the refinery in Springs. He was also from a solid, middle-class background and he was the first non-white person to work there as an engineer. Pravin had to move into "the Indian part of town", because although he was a graduate employee, apartheid meant the company was not allowed to house him. Pravin quickly became part of the fabric of the company. He was brilliant, enthusiastic and interested, and he contributed to many ambitious projects. A humble man, Pravin wanted to give back to the community where he lived. He was passionate about maths and science, so he decided to offer free maths and science classes to the local community.

Pravin identified one particular boy, Sifiso, as brilliant. Thanks, at least in part, to Pravin's support, Sifiso got an "A" in mathematics and a "B" in Physics when he passed his final school exams. Pravin was deeply impressed and persuaded the company to sponsor Sifiso's third-level education. Sifiso qualified as a chemical engineer at the University of Cape Town in December 2001 and started working at the company in January 2002.

Sifiso rose through the ranks at the refinery where his engaging personality and ability to work with people were as important to his progress as his exceptional mind and technical competence. After a few years, he made an unusual move, leaving the typical career track of a chemical engineer and moving first into finance, and then into sales and marketing. Sifiso is now a group executive in the company, responsible for the refinery as well as sales and marketing channels. He sits on the Group Executive Committee and works out of an office at the refinery in Springs, overlooking the township where he grew up.

His mentor Pravin is proud beyond measure of his *protégé*. Pravin too has been successful throughout his career and today manages the platinum and precious metal extraction operations at the refinery, considered one of the best in the world.

South Africa is full of stories like this, where corporates and individuals support communities. Irrespective of race or class, if one person can touch the life of another, and motivate and inspire that person to work, to achieve, and to become an educated professional, that is enough. I am sure that in giving lessons in the community Pravin inspired many to learn maths and science, and Sifiso's story is a particularly poignant example of his impact on society and the lives of people around him.

Celebrating Diversity

Sometimes it feels like we are so busy fulfilling the requirements imposed through South Africa's BBBEE codes that we forget there are good reasons to celebrate diversity, particularly in corporate teams.

BBBEE stands for Broad Based Black Economic Empowerment and all companies in South Africa are required to fulfil the code's directives in terms of ownership, management, suppliers, training opportunities, and other business areas. It is an aggressive affirmative action process, implemented at the end of apartheid in 1994 and adapted many times since then.

Unfortunately, BBBEE is not delivering on its promise. A recent McKinsey study showed that despite many years of BBBEE, we in South Africa still have a lot to do.

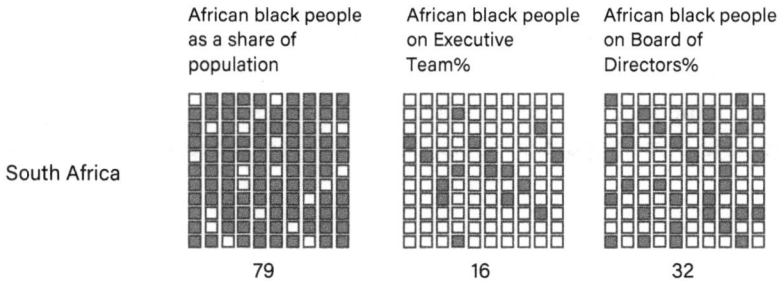

Figure 3: McKinsey Quarterly "Delivering through diversity" report, January 2018

BBBEE is seen as restitution for the evils of the past and, while restitution is important, terms like "previously disadvantaged", true as they are, might not always help us when it comes to celebrating diversity and the many good reasons for embracing it.

Here are just a few.

Financial and team success: An article in *The Economist* in November 2019 pointed out that it is hard to correlate diverse leadership with financial success. Companies that are more diverse may be more enlightened in ways that lead to their financial success, but it's hard to prove. What can be proven is that teams of surgeons do better when they are diverse. And a very recent *Harvard Business Review* study was able to demonstrate that in the venture capital sector, teams that had gender or ethnic diversity were markedly better at deal-making.

Another McKinsey report shows that gender diversity is particularly impactful at the executive team level. Groups with more women deliver better EBITDA (earnings before interest, taxes, depreciation, and amortisation) performance across the globe. This differential is even more apparent when the women are in line roles actually running business operations than when they are in staff roles such as HR or finance. This is key, as often we see women restricted to those staff roles on the executive committee rather than driving the operational business.

Innovation: There is no doubt about this one. Diverse teams are more innovative. Having the ability to frame questions from different perspectives brings real and positive change in organisations. Groupthink happens when an organisation is too homogenous: when, for example, everyone comes from a similar background in terms of race, culture and education. Although it might feel quicker and more efficient, groupthink impedes innovation and may also allow for bad behaviour to continue unchecked because it is culturally engrained in the organisation.

Higher employee satisfaction: Repeated studies show that organisations that successfully diversify – caring about their staff and implementing meaningful programmes to integrate and develop women, minority and ethnic groups – have happier and harder-working employees.

Enhanced awareness of bias: Behavioural economics has shown us that we are all subject to bias, mostly unconscious. This can limit our ability to analyse data and definitely has an impact on our decision making. People with different frameworks and viewpoints can help us to acknowledge and address our biases.

Breaking down homophily: One of our unconscious biases is known as homophily. This is, quite simply, the desire to associate with people like ourselves and it is linked to our deep-seated need to belong. Homophily can leave a lot of money on the table. In a study of venture capitalists, the venture capitalist industry was found to be "staggeringly" homogeneous. It found too that the few diverse venture capitalist teams were significantly better performers. If you strive for diversity, you will deliver results.

Women in Leadership

This is such a thorny topic that I hesitated to include it in this book.

Why is it so tricky? Study after study shows that women are not treated equally in the workplace. We earn less for a start. If we are good we often get tagged with descriptions of being tough and unpleasant. A deep and unpleasant vein of sexism runs through the corporate world. Let me be clear, I am not talking about #metoo and sexual abuse. I am taking about the everyday treatment of professional women, here in South Africa where I live and also in the many other countries where I have worked.

What's going on?

In Sheryl Sandberg's book *Lean In* she cited a study that described a successful venture capitalist, her career and her success. They then gave it to students and asked them to say what they thought about her. And here's the thing Half of the students got a description of her career with the name Heidi. And half with the name Howard. The students rated Heidi and Howard as equally successful, but while they found Howard likeable and inspiring, they disliked Heidi and "would not want to hire her or work with her."

That is mind-blowing when you think about it, but not surprising.

Add some more complexity to that, here in South Africa, by imagining Heidi as a woman of colour and you'll find a whole new layer of complexity in the answer. I have recently heard of two corporate CEOs bullying women of colour in public on their male-dominated executive committees. Why? These are senior women, extremely talented and successful. Yet they allow themselves to be put down in public and don't seem to have the tools to deal with it. What's wrong with us? That's the wrong question. What's wrong with those men? Maybe that's the wrong question. What's wrong with society and with business culture? That's a better question.

In growing up I had the good fortune to be treated exactly the same as my two brothers by my father and I think that has always helped me in my professional relationships with men. In fact, he probably pushed me more because he saw I had potential and clumsy social skills. Not all women were given this equal treatment and unconscious sexism probably starts in childhood, in the home.

When I started in business I think lack of confidence made me come across as rather arrogant and I made some huge mistakes with people. But I learned from them. And as I was good at the work itself, which has always been my saving grace, I still got promotions and a solid career path.

In my 30s, as a young consultant, I was quite badly bullied by older more established male consultants and initially I fought back. I learned that for me, this approach didn't work. Luckily, I was supported by some mentors with exceptional people skills, whom I could learn from, and I realised that the best approach for me is a friendly, warm style, with absolute clarity around boundaries. If someone tries to put me, or any other woman, down in a professional situation, I will call them on it, every time. But nicely.

Sexism, like racism, is probably subconscious. Men don't understand why we take offence because it's always been that way and it's normal to them. One of my South African colleagues told me that in her culture men look at women who are senior in business and think "who do you think you are?" She's outstandingly good at her job, but she says that men in her culture still think that women belong at home.

The irony is that all the studies show that businesses with diversity in their senior leadership roles do better. Better still when women are in the operational roles.

What can we do about this? Well, we are not going to change it, at least not in our generation of leaders. So, we must work with it. My suggestion is that women who are in senior roles must have the confidence to take their place at the table. We know you are good. You wouldn't be in the role you hold if you were not good. Have a point of view, and don't be afraid to share it. Invest in your development across the board. Make sure you have a view on the world as well as your business and the markets, no matter what role you hold.

Work hard at controlling your emotions, particularly when you feel bullied or put down. Bullies relish a response; if their darts appear not to wound, they will back off.

How to control your emotions? One very good way is to use a technique called distancing. Mentally step away from the table and observe what is going on as if it were happening to someone else. Ask yourself, how would I advise a friend to behave in this moment? This isn't easy, but you can train your brain to get better at self-observation. Practise it when you don't need it so that it's available to you when you do.

Remember what Victor Frankl said in *Man's Search for Meaning*: "Between stimulus and response there is a space. In that space is our power to choose our response. In our response lies our growth and our freedom." To put it more simply: it's not what happens, it's how you handle it that counts. In any given situation you always have a choice about how you handle it.

I see this bullying in the boardroom and in the executive committee so often that I am certain that it exists throughout organisations. If you are bullied or put down or made to feel uncomfortable in public, take it offline and have a conversation with that person. Remember, it may be unconscious on their part, so your job is to help them by making them aware of what is acceptable behaviour and what is not. I recommend doing this nicely, and in a one-on-one meeting.

We should support one another as women. And we should not demonise men. Yes, sexism runs deep; deeper in some cultures than others. As with racism if we just take that and resent it, we'll never move forward. You can resent the fact that men largely rule the world, and definitely the world of work. Or you can accept that as a woman, if you want to have a successful career, you need to learn to operate in that world of men, without losing the authenticity of who you are. That's not easy and it may not be fair, but if you want to be successful that's what you have to do.

Ethical Leadership

In February 2018 I had a great week. I started my new business, The Woodburn Mann Leadership Science Institute, and South Africa's top business book publishing house was keen to publish my first book *Find Your Focus: 5 steps to your best year ever.*

I had also been researching ethical leadership for a client who wanted to find a reliable corruption-assessment tool for leaders. My client has big businesses in sub-Saharan Africa and he's been burned by a few of his CEOs. We came up with a powerful model to address the issue, a unique assessment methodology purely focused on an executive's ethical leadership profile.

Ethics may seem a dull topic, but it's one I've loved since studying moral philosophy as an undergraduate at Trinity College, Dublin. Now we can benefit from research over the past 10 years that has increased our understanding of which factors, behaviours and traits may influence ethical behaviour.

As I dug into the research I began to see an overlap between specific leadership profiles and the traits and behaviours of well-known ethical leaders. The problem is, the findings show that people are most influenced by the ethical behaviour of the leader closest to them, not the leader at the top of the business. The challenge is to integrate ethical leadership into the culture and then cascade it down into the business.

Ethical behaviour is influenced by a number of factors including:

- The degree of sophistication in ethical thinking because ethical choices and conflicts of interest occur more often than we may realise

- The degree to which ethics have been embedded in organisational culture
- The context in which ethical choices occur
- The behaviour of an individual's direct leader
- The degree of social intelligence and empathy of the leader
- The humility of the person concerned, with less humility correlating to less honesty and ethical decision making.

All of the above are worthy of attention, but the issue of context is particularly worthy. Behavioural economics shows us how anchoring directly influences behaviour. To give you an example of anchoring, in a famous study, a photograph of eyes watching you by an "honesty" coffee bar greatly increased the contributions to the coffee. And the more threatening the eyes, the more money was collected. This study has been repeated many times. Similarly, seeing bad ethical behaviour unconsciously causes us to behave badly, though most of us would be loath to admit the truth of that.

In South Africa, a country where corruption is notoriously rife, not enough attention is paid to these simple points. Like many things, ethical behaviour is improved by learning. Ethical leadership programmes would be a sound additional to the arsenal of any CEO or Chief of People.

Part 4

WELLBEING

Loss and Grief

Loss and the consequent grieving process are not well understood. Most only find out about it when someone they love dies. Tragic as it is, they mourn and they learn about grieving. In some cases, though, the loss might be something incredibly important, rather than someone. Losses like these are more ephemeral and it can be harder to recognise that you may be grieving. I suspect it is a problem we are all facing as I write this during the 2020 Coronavirus pandemic. Those of us who are locked down are grieving the loss of the life we have known and we are uncertain of what the future holds.

Another problem is not realising the risk of "getting stuck in the grieving process". Recently I coached someone who had make a big career mistake. For years, his life was stuck because he had not come to terms with that mistake and its ramifications. Realising he was grieving for the death of his career was a huge revelation for him, a kind of liberation, and he has made great progress since then.

The grieving process is generally considered to have five steps and they are:

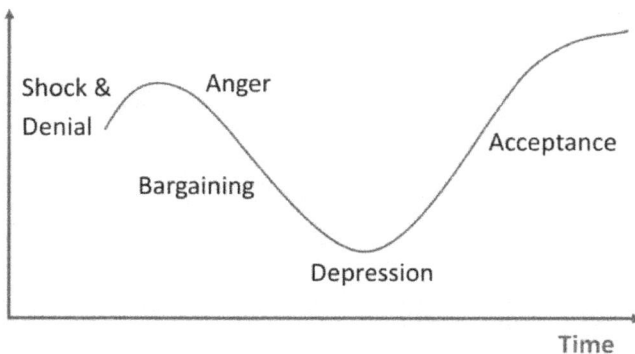

Figure 4: The Kübler-Ross framework for processing grief

In these cases, as with the loss of a loved one, the hardest part may the first step. We are in denial because to admit the truth can bring the whole, potentially shameful, truth crashing down upon us.

Only when you have accepted the loss can you start moving through the process of grieving for your loss. The grieving process is not linear – you might find yourself stuck or falling back a step. But it is a process and we do get through it.

This is important: Whether it is the death of a loved one, losing a job, or being forced to change your way of life, as in divorce or the time of coronavirus, every loss is different and affects every person in a different way. This framework is a useful tool to help describe a huge morass of messy human emotions.

There are books and dissertations written about this, but here are the key points:

Denial: Denial helps us to cope. One author says there is "grace in denial". But eventually denial is no longer possible.

Anger: This one is really messy. We recognise anger because we are used to it, and it has no limits. We can easily direct it at someone, even if it's not the right person. Underneath the anger lies your pain. You may be good at suppressing anger rather than feeling it, or you direct it elsewhere. The depth of your anger reflects the intensity of your love for what you have lost. Anger also has direction, in a way that denial does not – it gives you structure and a bridge to the next stage.

Bargaining: "If I do this, maybe I can change the outcome." This is particularly relevant, when you'd much rather not deal with the loss. One of the classic patterns in this case is to fall into the pattern of "if only". "If only I had been a better wife/friend/employee I would still have my husband/friendship/job." Bargaining is a part of the process, and probably one that will trip you up and take you right back to the start again.

Depression: This is really important. Depression in this process is like any depression in its symptoms but it is NOT a sign of mental illness. It is normal. It is an appropriate response. If you've never been depressed before you might feel really bad. If you have already experienced depression, what Winston Churchill used to call the "black dog" that sat between him and the world, you might not feel quite so bad. That said, depression is really, really awful, so even mild depression feels terrible. Again, it helps to understand what is happening. I am not a psychologist, but I can give you a personal opinion based on my own experience of grief and loss. It is this: if grief is a process of healing, then depression is a necessary part of that healing process.

Acceptance: This is about accepting that what you thought you had is gone, and maybe never even existed. That's hard to do. Acceptance doesn't mean you have to think it's ok, or even right. But it's not going to change, and when we realise that, and start to live with that, while we might never be ok with it, we start to come to terms with our grief and to move on.

Man's Search For Meaning
–Viktor Frankl

I would hesitate to compare the life of a CEO to life in the Nazi concentration camps if it were not for the fact that in his memoir Viktor Frankl gives us permission to do that very thing. To take lessons from the camps and apply them to our daily lives. When a man has been stripped of everything he possesses: freedom; dignity; food and drink; strength; health; and so much more, yet has the courage to survive and find hope in small things, we can learn from him.

As a reader of this book, I imagine your life probably has plenty of great moments. When the numbers in your business go well. When your people step up. When you get a chance to spend time with family or friends, or make time for skiing, riding, swimming, running or anything else you enjoy.

That said, your work may be relentless and you probably feel there is never enough time. All of this reduces your freedom, your control of your own destiny and, in a form of vicious cycle, can affect your ability to use the time you do have in the best way.

Frankl tells us that:

> *Everything can be taken from a man but one thing; the last of the human freedoms – to choose one's attitude in any given set of circumstances, to choose one's ways.*

> *Between stimulus and response there is a space. In that space is our power to choose our response. In our response lies our growth and freedom.*

Life does not work out as planned: it's an unrelenting series of problems. Yet, says Frankl,

It does not matter what we expected from life, but rather what life expected from us.

Our response to the questions of life is the right action and the right conduct.

No man and no destiny can be compared with any other man and any other destiny.

This journey is yours alone and incomparable. It calls on you to shape your own fate. Suffering is to be got through and problems need to be solved. This is part of the meaning of life.

Frankl explains why behaviour is so much more important than words.

The right example is more effective than words could ever be... The immediate influence of behaviour is always more effective than that of words.

Which is a positive if the immediate behaviour is good, but very difficult if the behaviour is poor or toxic.

Remember that managing the leaving of this "prison", be it grief or loss or any other deeply disturbing experience, is as important as anything else that you do. The relief of this intense pressure is the "psychological equivalent of the bends [a condition suffered by divers who surface too quickly]." Bitterness and disillusion are both possible when you end this journey, and of course it depends how it ends. But with time, they pass, and all that is left is memory, dissolving the worst of times to merely a dream.

Meditation

Research in neuroscience shows that the ancient Hindus were onto something. When you meditate you give your brain a rest. Lots of people meditate; it might surprise you who they are. Who knew that the "Governator" himself, Arnold Schwarzenegger, was once a devotee of transcendental meditation?

I'm not particularly good at meditating myself, and I struggle with mindfulness, unless I'm on a horse. But here's the thing that's connected me with trying to meditate. It turns out that even very short bursts of meditation help your brain a lot. I'm finding this to be true.

Though I would never claim to be as busy as a CEO, I do have the same "A-type" personality, so it can be hard for me to take a moment to pause. But now, when can't sleep, which is quite often, instead of stressing, I focus on trying to meditate. The result is that even if I am not meditating very well, I know the attempt is good for my brain, and it takes my mind off not sleeping.

How to meditate

Here's how:

Close your eyes and focus your attention on your breathing. Breathe in for three counts. Hold for three counts. Breathe out for three counts. Still for three counts. Breath in for three counts... continue to concentrate entirely on your breathing and the counting.

When your mind wanders, don't worry about it, notice it, and calmly draw your attention back to focus back to your breathing and start again. There's no right or wrong. Just doing this for 30 seconds is good for your brain. If you are awake and you are very stressed, set your phone alarm for 30 seconds and do this. Try a minute.

This is one of the biggest presents you can give your brain. You won't notice any immediate effect but over time you will feel calmer. You may sleep better and even if you don't, while you lie awake, you give your brain the break it needs.

Apps are wonderful support for meditation. My preferred app is called Insight Timer and has lots of free meditations of varying lengths. Many people like Calm, though they do charge a fee for their best content. Another recommendation from editor and friend Sophie Kevany is an app called Headspace.

On Sleep

Tiredness impacts on your energy levels and your performance. So it's time to talk about sleep. This is personal, rather than leadership based, yet essential to the daily quality of your performance. What follows is basically a set of guidelines I have developed that might be worth building into both home and travel routines.

There is a revolution going on about the importance of sleep. To the point where Amazon CEO Jeff Bezos recently told Ariana Huffington, editor of the Huffington Post, that he now demands eight hours of rest. As he put it, "If I make half of the decisions, but they're 5% better, that's better for Amazon."

Recent research on sports has shown that recovery and sleep are two of the four ingredients that enhance sporting performance (note that the other two are nutrition and mindset). The same is likely to be true for your performance as an executive.

Understanding more about sleep may help you to enhance the quality of the sleep you get.

How much is enough?

We used to be proud of how little sleep we needed. We'd boast about pulling all-nighters and running on four hours' sleep. Now we know that operating on four hours sleep can be compared to arriving drunk at work. Exactly. That means a CEO running on just a few hours' sleep might be as good as drunk.

The ideal sleep time is seven to eight hours a night, but this is only a guideline. Some do well on slightly more, some on slightly less.

Why sleep?

The more we know about sleep, the more we are discovering that natural sleep is a wonder drug. Just a few of the benefits of a good night's sleep include: better stress processing; immune system relief; greater self-control and benefits for both diet and exercise. Memories are laid down too and this is a huge one as lack of sleep can have a major impact on memory and decision-making. At the same time, the toxins associated with Alzheimer's are washed away in sleep and inflammation is reduced. In short, we are brighter and better when we get the sleep we need.

Sleep aids

I use sleeping pills in certain circumstances: when I travel, when I'm in pain, or when I'm very anxious. This is because I find it very hard to perform well when sleep deprived. Long-term use of any sleeping pills is not healthy and I try to limit my own use to emergencies or when I am travelling. I stick to zolpidem (Stilnox or Ivedal), and never ever take loprazolam (Dormonoct). The last is a benzodiazepine which makes it highly addictive.

My personal decision is to take the medication when I absolutely have to, and, at the same time, cultivate good sleep hygiene so that I need medication less and less.

Sleep hygiene

Sleep hygiene is the term used to describe the healthy routines that help you get to sleep. A hot shower or a bath, a dark room. Blue light emanating from screens is thought to be the enemy of sleep so no blue light in the room. That means turning all screens off or at least putting them onto "night shift" mode and keeping the phone well away from the bed. No reading from screens after you've got into bed, unless you turn off blue light. Paper is better. Routine is your best friend. Waking up at the same time every day is important.

When you have intense days you may not be able to turn off the buzz when you go to bed. Natural products that might help are chamomile tea, pumpkin seed oil and melatonin. Some people find milky drinks helpful, which might sound childlike, but if it works, who cares? Another natural remedy is two tablespoons of apple cider vinegar and one tablespoon of honey in a cup of hot water. Fermented foods, and liquids like vinegar, are very good for us and aid digestion, which might in turn help sleep. Tim Ferriss, author of *The Four Day Week*, swears by this one. I often have it before I go to bed and indeed it may help.

My best sleeping aid is the Audible App from Amazon. Audible has increased the number of books I get through in the year, which is great. Even better there is a sleep timer and I find if I wake up during the night and set the timer to eight minutes, I am usually asleep before the timer runs out. If I'm not, at least I have something interesting to listen to rather than lying awake worrying about something that simply won't seem important in the morning which has always been my default.

Part 5

STRATEGY AND DECISION MAKING

Strategy and Purpose

The strategy tells you WHAT the business does, and HOW it's going to do it.

But it doesn't tell you WHY the business does what it does.

People don't buy into "What?" and "How?", they buy into **belief** – into understanding why you are doing what you do. If you can capture that 'Why', use it to drive the business, and its marketing and hiring strategies, then you have a strategy that puts that belief at the centre of everything you do. That is incredibly powerful, in good part because it provides a solid basis for decision-making and communications.

The concept of "Why" has been explained brilliantly by Simon Sinek in one of the most popular Ted Talks ever called "Start with Why".

Because CEOs often prefer their information in five-minute chunks, here's a YouTube link to a five minute summary of Sinek's talk. It will take less than that to see what he's getting at.

> **You Tube** Simon Sinek, Start with Why, retrieved from: https://www.youtube.com/watch?v=IPYeCltXpxw

Decisions and Judgement

My favourite author of the 21st Century is Daniel Kahneman, founder of Behavioural Economics, winner of the Nobel prize for Economics and author of *Thinking Fast and Slow*, a book that has had a profound effect on sport, the military and the world of business.

In a recent podcast, Kahneman shared his thoughts on negotiation, decision-making and judgement. Here's a summary:

Negotiation: if you want to get someone from point A to point B, pressure doesn't work. Pressure is persuasion, promises or threats. We tend to push our negotiation "opponents" by using what we think are the best driving forces. Instead, try counter-intuitive thinking and ask yourself: "Why are they not at point B already?" Figuring out the answer to that helps to remove the barriers and restraining forces.

Kahneman calls this "the greatest idea in psychology".

Judgement: Be slower to judge people. Behaviour is less a reflection of personality than of situation. Many factors cause people to behave as they do: good motivations can lead to bad behaviour; bad motivations can lead to good behaviour. Kahneman believes that we should be less swift to judge personality based on behaviour in any given situation.

Making decisions: We are so driven by our biases that we constantly make and justify poor decisions. Some ideas from Kahneman:

Break decisions down into their component parts, analyse them and score them. Finally, when you have done that, close your eyes and ask what your intuition says. This delays your intuitive judgement until you have an analysis of all the facts; then your intuition will be a powerful and reliable tool. Most people first make an intuitive judgement immediately, then use the "facts" to support their bias.

Organisations make better decisions than people. In many cases algorithms make the best decisions. This links to Ray Dalio's approach to investment decisions. Ray Dalio is the co-chief investment officer of Bridgewater Associates which he founded in 1975 and which is one of the most successful investment companies in the world. He has a brilliant logical mind and the ability to convert his thinking processes into algorithms using a methodology that he describes in his book *Principles*. Most of us can't do that, but we can develop personal and organisational processes that drive better decisions.

Seek feedback and innovative thinking. Kahneman says we must protect our dissenters. They are your most valuable people. Best of all run "pre-mortems". Just before you make an important decision everyone involved must take a blank sheet of paper and answer the following: "It's two years from now and this decision failed. What is the history of that failure?" As big decisions, like deals or large capital investments, gather momentum and support, it can get harder and harder for dissenters to have a voice. Instead of being useful, questions become annoying. The process of pre-mortems gives everyone a voice and forces even the supporters to step back, broaden their perspective and see a wider range of choices. For important decisions this can be invaluable.

A leadership paradox: One of the paradoxes of leadership is that slowing down our decision-making and judgement makes us better and more thoughtful leaders. But people don't like deliberative leaders, they see them as lacking in confidence. They like leaders who are intuitive because speed and intuition denote confidence.

Distilling Extreme Ownership

Sports and some military organisations (notably the US and UK) have been early adopters of many of the research-based concepts that I discuss in this book. These are the same concepts we use to develop executive performance when working with our clients. Corporate business has been a laggard in terms of applying the new science of performance to executive leadership and leadership throughout the organisation, and is only now opening up to these concepts. Sporting teams and military training commanders picked up on this research as far back as the early 2000s and have been refreshing and refining their approaches ever since, as new research emerges.

Jocko Willink and Leif Babin's share how the US Navy Seals use these concepts in their brilliant book *Extreme Ownership,* which takes lessons they learned during deployment in the Iraq war and applies them to the world of business. They espouse a set of principles that, frankly, all truly great leaders tend to adopt. I know from my discussions with CEOs over the years that every one of these will resonate with them.

A couple of years after *Extreme Ownership* Willink and Babin published a new book, *The Dichotomy of Leadership.* In it they said they stood by everything they had said in their first book, except that it had one problem. The title.

Why? Because, as they point out, everything in leadership is about balance. That means that any extreme, even extreme ownership, would lead to a bad result, every time. They also said the concept of extreme ownership could be misconstrued to imply that the leader owns everything that happens and therefore has to be involved with everything that happens. That's not the case. Not in the military, not in business. The role of the leader is to empower others to own all these principles, to live by them. And to have employees' backs when it goes wrong. You don't have to be it all and do it all. In fact, beyond creating a leadership culture, making the principles clear so that others can apply them, and ensuring that employees feel safe, the less leaders do the better.

The principles described in Extreme Ownership are the following:

1. Leaders take Extreme Ownership: this is the essence of true leadership when it is applied to oneself. Leadership starts with self and in that context extreme ownership is a *sine qua non*

2. There are no bad teams, only bad leaders: the story told in this chapter is one of my favourite leadership stories ever. I will be telling it for years.

   Willink was running a training course for US Navy Seals candidates. The trainers became invested in the success of the candidates, so it was really tough on them when candidates failed. In this training exercise, the participants were on the beach, divided into six teams each consisting of six men. Each team had to pick up a heavy WWII wooden boat, carry it down to the water, row a course of buoys, return to the shore, then carry the boat to the finish line.

   This was a long training session. They ran the race again and again, changing the course each time. As time went by a trend set in. Team Two consistently won. Team Six consistently lost. The whole of Team Six risked failing the training session and the whole programme. The trainers got together and thought about what to do. They came up with a simple solution. They changed the leaders of the two teams.

   In the next race guess what happened? Team Six won. Leadership is everything. Always.

   How did the Team Leader do it? By implementing a leadership concept known as "Small Wins". Instead of bullying and harrying the men to go faster, he set small goals throughout the race. Picking the boat up quickly, running it to the shoreline fast, casting off efficiently, finding the best course to the first buoy, and so on throughout each small step of the race. By achieving smaller goals, the men grew in confidence; they started to focus and perform. And win.

3. Believe

4. Check the ego

5. Cover and move: teamwork, breaking down silos and understanding the interdependencies

6. Simplify

7. Prioritise and execute

8. Decentralised command

9. Plan

10. Leading up and down the chain of command

11. Decisiveness (and uncertainty)

12. Discipline equals freedom

Part 6

PEOPLE

On Leadership Capital

Excerpt From: Jocko Willink and Leith Babin (ex-UK Navy Seal): *The Dichotomy of Leadership*

> *Leaders, on the one hand, cannot be too lenient. But on the other hand, they cannot become overbearing. They must set high standards and drive the team to achieve those standards, but they cannot be domineering or inflexible on matters of little strategic importance. To find this balance, leaders must carefully evaluate when and where to hold the line and when to allow some slack. They must determine when to listen to subordinate leaders and allow them ownership, making adjustments for their concerns and needs.*

I love the work of Jocko Willink and Leith Babin. They were Navy Seals who saw some of the toughest times in the Iraq war and their books bring the experience in the battlefield to the world of business. I introduced them in an earlier blog[8] and mentioned that sports and the military have been far quicker to adopt new thinking about leadership and wellbeing than the world of business, and these two authors have an engaging way of bridging the gap between the world of war and the world of business.

My sport is the equestrian sport of eventing and, for me, the best part is the cross country, but it's also the scariest part. Everything is built on confidence, and the connection between horse and rider. I was invited to do a "course walk" at Badminton in England, the very apotheosis of the sport, led by Virginia (Ginny) Elliot, who has won there several times and is one of the eventing world's greats. I loved the way she talked about "money in the bank" as you go round the track. When you do a good jump, with no mistakes, it's "money in the bank", said Ginny. When you have a messy jump, for any reason, it's a "withdrawal

---

8   See blog on "Distilling Extreme Ownership", page 66.

from the bank". The bank referred to is confidence – yours and more importantly, the horse's. If you are having a bad day, you make too many withdrawals you will either fall, or your horse will choose not to jump, so you will be eliminated. Willink and Babin talk about leadership capital in a similar way, and Stephen Covey uses the same analogy when he talks about relationship capital.[9]

Leadership capital

Willink and Babin use the term "leadership capital" as a means to understand the careful analysis required for a leader to balance the dichotomy between leniency and strength. Very similar to Ginny's description of "money in the bank", leadership capital is the recognition that there is a finite amount of power that any leader possesses. It can be expended foolishly by leaders who harp on matters that are trivial and strategically unimportant. Such capital is acquired slowly, by building trust and confidence with teams and by demonstrating that the leader has the long-term good of the team and their mission in mind. Prioritising those areas where standards cannot be compromised, and holding the line there while allowing for some slack in other, less critical areas is a wise use of leadership capital.

───────────────

9   See blog on "The 7 Habits of Highly Effective People, Part three – Habits 4 – 6", page 100.

Potential

In one of my client interactions I noticed that a succession crunch was coming. Although I only saw a small snapshot of the business, I could see that a lot of the senior leaders were older than the CEO himself. Who was going to take over when they left?

HR was never considered strategic in that business, and talent development was not on the agenda. The most senior executives lacked knowledge about management and leadership development even as their own talent and ability shone through.

How do you change this? There are many possibilities. One is to create a high potential programme in the business so that talented people can be retained and groomed for future leadership. Study after study shows that this type of long-term talent thinking is one of the key contributors to a company's success.

One of the most important objectives when developing talent is to assess not only current competencies but the *potential* for further development, which is much harder to do.

Knowledge and current ability are one thing, potential is another. High-potential programmes put in place the development opportunities that are needed to close that gap. These include education, coaching and stretch assignments.

Who's going to lead? A short series on hiring and growing talent

Some say the CEO is really the CRO (Chief Recruitment Officer). It's true; if you can recruit and promote A players, you get an A team.

- You need to SOURCE great candidates

- You need to KNOW what you want them to do

- You need to ASSESS them against those criteria

- Finally, you need to be able to SELL them on your vision

I've seen many clients hire great talent without a clear idea of what the job is. For every role it is essential to work out exactly what the job involves, so that you can assess candidates against very precise needs. There's no point in hiring a great all-rounder if what you need is someone who will lead your talent development initiative. They also need to be the right cultural fit and have the competencies to do the job.

Culture

They say that "culture eats strategy for breakfast[10]". Have you ever done an evaluation or analysis of your culture? You can pay consultants a fortune to do this. Or you can do a quick pulse check yourself.

Get your team together and ask them to give you adjectives that describe the culture as it is now. Some negative words like "hierarchical, culture of fear, bullying" might come up, but there will be lots of positives too. Capture them all. It's a brainstorm so let the discussion run, no criticism. Ask them to be honest. Then ask them to describe the culture

---

10   This quote is often attributed to Peter Drucker. However further investigation reveals that he died (in 2005) before the first recorded use of this quote in 2011.

you want to build. Some of the same words will come up, but hopefully some different ones as well, ones that might indicate a new direction: "a company with heart" for example.

Now look at your team. You know they can survive in the current culture. But have they got what it takes to thrive as an A-player in a different culture? Do some of them need development or coaching to bridge that gap?

When you hire new people make sure that they can operate in the current culture, but that their values lie in the culture you want to build.

Who? Identifying A-Players

What does an A-player look like? One thing we know is that the way people have behaved in the past is a good indicator of how they will behave in the future. To assess those behaviours, we use competencies. Competencies indicate how someone will operate in a role and achieve the desired (hopefully well-defined) outcomes.

When I assess CEO candidates, it's this competency assessment that enables me to describe to a board what will happen to the business if they hire candidate X or candidate Y. I assess candidates on a scale of one to eight, and CEO candidates should score 5+ on the critical competencies. There is plenty of long-term, hard-core research that supports the validity of competencies as a predictor of future behaviour.

A-players need to be outstanding in the following critical competencies. If members of your "A" team are poor at any of these, you have a choice: find out if they can be developed? Or make changes to your team.

In no particular order:

- Efficiency
- Honesty and integrity
- Organisation and planning
- Follow-through on commitments (which is for me the very definition of integrity)
- Assertive and determined (strong and courageous without being abrasive)
- Analytic intelligence and strategic thinking
- Attention to detail
- Persistence

- Proactivity (takes the initiative)
- Emotional intelligence (which includes an ego low enough to listen to others and take feedback)
- Social intelligence

There are other competencies that matter for particular roles and situations – especially competencies around leadership, management and the ability to create followership. But the list above is the *sine qua non* and A-players should rate high in all of them.

Who? Hiring A-Players

> *Executives owe it to the organisation and to their fellow workers
> not to tolerate non-performing individuals in important jobs.*
> —Peter Drucker

A CEO that I work with told me that he wants to be surrounded by excellent people and give them the authority to be autonomous in their work.

I asked him the following questions:

- Does everyone in your business understand and agree with your position?
- Is HR driven by these core philosophies?
- Do the people on your team recruit A-players? What about the people on their teams?
- Do young leaders in the business understand what it takes to be an A-player?
- Do they know where their own gaps are and how to grow?

> *If each of us hires people who are smaller than we are, we shall
> become a company of dwarfs. But if each of us hires people who
> are bigger than we are, we shall become a company of giants.*
> David Ogilvy

Five things to think about when recruiting A-players

Build a pipeline of A-players and use the network. Keep an eye out for exceptional executives. When you find them, make a note of them. Encourage your top team to do the same. If the companies you partner with come across someone outstanding and don't have a role for them, encourage them to send that person your way. Do the same for them.

Hire diversity in race and gender. We tend to recruit in our own image[11] but businesses do better when they have diverse leadership teams. Diverse teams have better collective judgement and make better decisions. On a side note, businesses are more innovative when they have more women in research and development roles[12]. Make sure to check that your hiring team or agency understands your quest for diversity and why it's so important.

Sell them: A-players have choices; you and your recruitment team need to be selling them throughout the process. Consider these aspects:

- Fit – sell them on your vision

- Family – what are the consequences for their family? What can you do to mitigate that?

- Freedom to operate – if you are hiring great people you don't have to micromanage them or manage them much at all

- Money – yes, they will want a good package but see the next point

- Fun – working with the best and creating something great should be fun; great thinking doesn't happen in a negative environment

Think about employee motivation. People are not motivated by money alone; there is a hierarchy of needs that drives motivation. Once our basic needs are in place things like belonging (to a successful team of like-minded people, for example), self-esteem and self-actualisation become part of motivation[13].

---

11 See blog on "Fear and Courage", page 2.

12 In a study published in *Innovation: Management, Policy & Practice*, the authors analysed levels of gender diversity in research and development teams from 4 277 companies in Spain. Using statistical models, they found that companies with more women were more likely to introduce radical new innovations into the market over a two-year period. These findings have been supported in additional studies.

13 This is derived from Maslow's hierarchy of needs. Often depicted as a triangle with psychological at the base followed by safety, love/belonging, esteem, with self-actualisation at the top of the triangle

Have an interviewing strategy. If you are disciplined about how you interview and take references to validate your findings, you are more likely to wean out B- and C-players and save time. Good interviewing techniques can also help address the tendency to hire in our own likeness as it puts the focus on skills and ability, rather than where a person is from or what they look or sound like.

> *In looking for people to hire, you look for three qualities: integrity, intelligence, and energy. And if you don't have the first, the other two will kill you. You think about it; it's true. If you hire somebody without [integrity], you really want them to be dumb and lazy.*
> —Warren Buffet

Shaping the Executive Team

People are always top of mind so here's some data from research done by Heidrick and Struggles on incoming CEOs and the Executive Team. For a short time during 2017 I worked with Heidrick & Struggles on projects and enjoyed the r data-based approach to 'the soft stuff'.

Why it's often best to take tough decisions sooner rather than later

New CEOs are likely to let go of senior executives when they step into the role. Most commonly relieved of their duties are the legal counsel, the chief marketing officer, the head of sales or the chief operating officer. No matter who goes, most CEOs wish they had made the decision to restructure the team sooner than they did.

First time CEOs may hesitate because they don't feel like they know enough and want to give people the benefit of the doubt. Experienced CEOs tend to act more quickly.

Keeping executives with negative energy does more harm than good, but even letting disruptive leaders go is not easy. They have talent and you need talent. But, the longer you wait to let them go, the more damage they will do and the greater the drag on the organisation.

According to Price and Toye there are seven archetypes of disruptive leaders:

- **The Troublemaker**: This is not the person who push boundaries, questions assumptions and helps the organisation to think outside the box. Troublemakers tend to be people who constantly create chaos and push boundaries in negative ways.

- **The Overpromiser/Underdeliverer**: Someone with an inflated self-image who makes boastful promises. If they can't deliver on the scale of their ego, it's a problem.

- **The Customer isn't King**: Customers are hard to gain and easy to lose. If a senior leader does not get that, you don't need them.

- **The Incapable**: If you've hired them to do a job, been clear about that job and given them the support they need to do it, they must do it. If they can't or won't, don't give them too many chances.

- **The Flake**: Some people look the part and talk the part and might even have the talent. But if they don't deliver consistently, or don't show up consistently, you can't trust them.

- **The Entitled**: Thin-skinned and entitled, they spend their time waiting for others to slip up and moan about it. They might even threaten legal action. Cut them loose.

- **The Insubordinate Subordinate**: Whatever the rules of conduct are, executives must adhere to them. If they don't (whether it's an employee being insubordinate to their boss, or a lie told on a CV) they must go.[14]

---

14 This list is derived from Price, C. and Toye, S., 2017. *Accelerating Performance: How Organizations Can Mobilize, Execute, and Transform with Agility.* John Wiley & Sons.

These are extreme cases, and most of the CEOs I work with wouldn't tolerate much of this behaviour on their team in any case. Some cases are less clear cut. For example, where someone was hired to do a job, and the job grew but they didn't. These people can be the hardest to let go because they delivered in the past and they fit with the culture. But they have to go and they may end up happier elsewhere.

Part 7

ROLE OF THE CEO

Reputation and Personal Brand

One of the topics of conversation that comes up as executives move into more senior roles is personal brand. We all have one, and very few of us manage it actively. If you are either CEO or an Executive Officer of a business, you should consider it. You may well decide that you want to stay "below the radar", which is fine, but I would still advise you to stay aware of how and where your name might be used. A simple way is to regularly google your own name, using a browser like Brave Browser with a history log you can fully delete. That will give you better and more accurate results. Everyone should do this.

Once you are in the top job, your personal brand is even more important because the image of a company and its CEO are inextricably entangled. The CEO's own brand and reputation matter to the company at many levels.

In recent studies reported in an article on Corporate Governance by Amrop, over 50% of senior executives believed that the CEO's personal reputation is of increasing importance to their company's reputation.

They also estimate that 44% of their company's market value can be attributed to CEO reputation. When we think about the impact that a crumbling CEO's reputation has on share prices, it is hard to disagree.

Most also believe that a positive reputation is significant in attracting investors, employees, and around half say it influenced their decision to join the organisation and to remain with it.

That sounds like a good thing, but it cuts both ways because part of how a message lands will inevitably be seen through the filters through which CEOs are perceived; the cloak of power if you like. The 2018 Edelman Trust Barometer[15] found that CEO credibility has jumped

---

15   2020 Edelman Trust Barometer. Retrieved from: https://www.edelman.com/trustbarometer

by seven points over that past year, with 44% rating CEOs as 'very credible'. Edelman puts this down to leaders "voicing their positions on the issues of the day." But 60% still think CEOs are driven "more by greed than a desire to make a positive difference in the world". The different perceptions, and knowing about them, are important, because they will influence how people interpret the CEO's actions.

For the CEO, cultivating your personal reputation enhances the reputation of the organisation. But what exactly goes into creating a good reputation and a solid personal brand?

Five drivers of reputation management

- How we are perceived. For example, our values, our credibility, trustworthiness, dependability, authenticity
- The positive motivations of the partners with whom we interact – negative stakeholders operating in bad faith can be damaging
- Our reaction to critical feedback, our ability to seek it out and how well we take it on board
- Significant life achievements, or missing achievements, and our relationship with these
- Our communication and self-marketing abilities

Some questions to think about when you consider your own reputation:

- Which life events, experiences, relationship etc., shaped my reputation?
- What is the essence of who I am and who I want to be seen as?
- Which observers and stakeholder groups are critical to building my reputation?
- Which personal characteristics are particularly important?

- What are the different elements of my reputation management? Do I manage my reputation in any way?

- How does my personal reputation influence that of my company?

- Which attributes or labels would third parties assign to my personal brand?

CEO Succession Planning – Case Study from a JSE Listed Company

Almost everyone would agree that the company board's most important job is CEO succession planning. But if so, why were so many South African boards caught out by a maelstrom of departing CEOs from major listed companies in 2019 with no successor in place? Examples include Eric Venter at Comair, Maria Ramos at ABSA, and Guy Hayward at Massmart.

According to research done by MIT Sloane there are three main reasons why boards fail at CEO succession planning. First, they fail to align succession planning parameters with the organisation's future strategic needs. Second, they are reluctant to upset the incumbent CEO by addressing succession planning. And third, they do not pay enough attention to developing the executives below the CEO and C-suite level.

Case study

In March 2019 the board of a JSE listed company asked our company, the Woodburn Mann Leadership Science Institute, to carry out a comprehensive CEO succession planning process. The Woodburn Mann Leadership Science Institute is led by consultants with extensive global experience in succession planning and our leadership framework is based on the most recent and relevant academic research.

Good succession planning rests on the consideration of multiple timeframes: What if your CEO decides to step down tomorrow, as she might, for a myriad of possible reasons? What if she leaves in three to five years? What if she stays for nine years? These timeframes mean the board needs to know who can step in immediately, if necessary, while considering the potential of key executives for medium- and long-term development to the CEO position.

In our business case, 'Strategic CEO Succession Planning at a JSE listed company", we look at how one company board decided to implement strategic CEO succession planning and the impact this had on business. Practical results included creating a "Readiness" panel of prospective talent, development plans for every member of the Executive Committee and their successors, and bold lateral career moves for some executives. A key success factor in this assignment was our partnership with the CEO and the Group Executive for People. Both invested time and energy and a true spirit of partnership to ensure a successful outcome.

The company s board was delighted with what we achieved and continues to actively support the ongoing development of C-Suite executives and their successors.

CEO pressures – long-termism versus short-termism

I'm not generally a great fan of "here's four things you can do to make your business succeed" but I came across an article in the *Harvard Business Review* which I thought might resonate. I've summarised the key points.

Short-termism

There's been a recent avalanche of studies and articles suggesting that CEOs focus too much on the short-term and chasing the next quarter's results. One study showed, however, that this doesn't have to be the case. It picked out four practices that help CEOs master the short-term while creating long-term social and economic value. These are:

Tell a story with purpose

If a CEO has a compelling narrative, investors will buy into it. Great stories are credible, simple, and consistent. They use both financial and non-financial metrics to link long-term vision, clear values, a distinctive business strategy, and focused operational priorities. Essential to the story is the company's purpose, and fundamental to that purpose is explaining why a company does what it does.

Set realistic targets

Don't sell pipe-dreams and spend every quarter chasing the impossible. If a CEO is open with shareholders about how long it might take for international expansion to deliver significant profits, they are far more likely to be patient.

Create lasting values

"Culture beats strategy"[16]. Companies that have a unique set of values, ranging from customer service, to engineering excellence and research brilliance are the most likely to garner investor support in tough times and withstand unwelcome takeover bids.

Innovate. Innovate. Innovate.

Ambitious innovation is key to survival. All the evidence supports it.

The article concludes that investors are perfectly willing to buy into long-termism, if the CEO succeeds in persuading them that it's worthwhile.

---

16 I have often see this is attributed to Peter Drucker but it appears he never actually said it.

What only the CEO can do

A.G. Lafley is one of the legends of American business, "the most lauded CEO in history"[17]. I regularly share my view that mistakes are learning opportunities Lafley went a step further, writing in the *Harvard Business Review* about how "I think of my failures as a gift".

My business partner Andrew Woodburn points out that CEOs spend too much of their time "fighting the fires of yesterday instead of sowing the crops that will bear fruit tomorrow."[18] CEOs need to hire great people so that they can focus on what only they can do.

Lafley had never been a CEO when he took the helm at P&G. His first few months were rough: the share price had fallen 30% and fell another 11% the week he was appointed. He led a complete recovery and transformation and is now seen as the greatest CEO P&G ever had. He wrote this article for the *Harvard Business Review* towards the end of his first 10-year stint, and I have summarised it here.

What the CEO should do

- Define the meaningful outside

- Decide what business you are in

- Balance present and future

- Shape values and standards

---

17 Reingold, J. 2016. *P&G Chairman A.G. Lafley Steps Down – For Good, This Time.* Retrieved from: https://fortune.com/2016/06/01/pg-chairman-a-g-lafley-steps-down-for-good-this-time/

18 Quote from Andrew Woodburn, my Partner in the Woodburn Mann Leadership Science Institute

Define the meaningful outside

Human nature means that people tend to focus internally. In an organisational context that means they tend to focus on internal systems, processes, people, and even values. The CEO has a clear perspective across the organisation and accountability to stakeholders, or, in other words, the company's external presence. Only a CEO can decide which external constituency matters most. External constituents include customers, regulators, competitors, unions, etc.

Deciding what business you are in

The CEO identifies the spaces where the company can win. Peter Drucker said "the CEO should decide what is our business; what should it be. Equally important, what is *not* our business and what *should* it *not* be." Only the CEO has the enterprise vision to make those tough choices.

Balancing present challenges and future opportunities

CEOs live with this one every day. As CEO you must make a choice between yield from present activities and investment in an unknown future.

Lafley also said that one of the most important decisions he made was to ensure that internal stretch goals were not confused with published goals, which must be much more realistic. The market will always like you if you deliver. Short term, this approach to goal setting might not be so popular, but it generally proves more reliable in the longer term.

Balancing present and future human resources is equally important. CEOs must have a keen understanding of their top talent and they should be personally involved in their development plans. If you are a CEO, this would be a good time to ask yourself: Have you identified high-potential managers? Are you spending personal time with the top 150 managers? Do you know how the business is investing in their growth?

Shaping values and standards

Values are about behaviour. Great values connect internal behaviour to the meaningful outside and are relevant now and in the future.

Standards are about expectations. They define what winning looks like. They answer the questions: "Do we know if we are winning with those who matter most (for example, the customer)? Are we winning against the very best?"

Part 8

HABITS (Revisited)

We were discussing *The 7 Habits of Highly Effective People* and my client said, "I must re-read it." "Tell you what," I replied. "I've got some time over Christmas. I'll read it and summarise it for you."

What follows is a four-part summary of the book.

The 7 Habits of Highly Effective People
–Stephen Covey

The best of The 7 Habits and is it still relevant?

First published 29 years ago, there are sections of the seven habits that are outdated. For example, our knowledge of neuroscience has totally changed how we think about the brain and makes the old left brain/ right brain thinking rather irrelevant. Covey's theory of paradigms is now much better understood through the biases and heuristics that have been identified by behavioural economics.

What hasn't changed are the concepts of self-management, integrity and principles, which I will discuss in the next few thought pieces. Nor the fact that we are capable of lifelong growth and development.

Covey himself said in an interview 25 years after the book was published: "I struggle with the habits every day. I'm not perfect, but I keep working on them."

What's it about again?

In another interview later in his life, after Covey had taught the principles in the book many times over the years he said: "You can pretty much summarise the first three habits with "make and keep a promise" and the next three with "involve others in the problem and work out the solution together." That's a great summary.

Some great quotes from The 7 Habits of Highly Effective People:

On values and principles

> We are building character, not personality.

Principles are territory, values are maps. So, your values can be false (a band of robbers shares values) unless they cohere with solid principles.

What are those principles? The most important are: fairness; integrity; human dignity; service to others; quality and excellence; potential and growth; patience, nurturance and encouragement.

Meditation and values can bring peace and spirituality. But be careful! They don't make you right!

On ownership, responsibility and growth

We are what we repeatedly do; excellence then is not an act but a habit.
—Aristotle, as quoted by Covey.

Covey points out that you are not just your habits, because you can change what you do.

It's not what happens, but how you handle it that counts.

In saying that we can choose our responses and that we must take ownership of the outcomes of our choices Covey cites Victor Frankl[19].

On management and leadership

Success is on the far side of failure
—Tom Watson, CEO, IBM 1914–1956
Management is doing the things right; leadership is doing the right thing.
—Peter Drucker

---

19   See blog on *Man's Search for Meaning* by Viktor Frankl, page 55.

For his own part, Covey advises us to "Organise and execute around priorities." To do this he uses the Eisenhower Matrix. See figure 5 for the Eisenhower matrix. I also describe it in detail in my book *Find Your Focus: 5 steps to your best year ever.*

On the seventh habit: continuous investment in personal growth

> *We are the instruments of our own performance and we need to recognise the importance of taking time regularly to sharpen the saw in all four ways. Physical, mental, social/emotional, spiritual.*

> *Almost all the benefit comes at the very end (of exercise). The same principle works on emotional muscles as well. Like patience, the fibre gets strong if you exercise it beyond past limits.*

Part Two – Habits 1 - 3

You can pretty much summarise the first three habits with 'make and keep a promise.'
–Stephen Covey

The 7 Habits are an inside-out process. We start with self-mastery and then move on to "teamwork, cooperation and communication".

The emphasis in the first three habits is on building character rather than attaining success.

In discussing character Covey talks about mental maps and paradigms. In the language of behavioural economics, we might talk about framing and how our cognitive blindness limits what we see and do. We also know that priming – basically the behaviour or event we have seen most recently – influences how we join the mental dots. The language may have changed but the principle stands.

When considering yourself, consider the output of which you are capable, what you want. Then consider the machine that produces that output – you, your physical and mental wellbeing and your character. Don't confuse the two. Covey calls these P for production (what you want) and PC for production capability (that's you). These must be balanced – if you burn out the PC, there won't be any P. If you invest in PC, you'll get the P. Covey says PC is the goose (us) and P is the golden eggs. We must look after the goose that lays the golden eggs!

Habit 1: Be proactive

Victor Frankl, who survived the Nazi Holocaust camps, said in describing how he endured those terrible years: "When we are no longer able to change a situation, we are challenged to change ourselves." This is often expressed as "It's not what happens to you, but how you handle

97

it that counts."

Habit 1 is about attitude. Our attitude defines how we respond to what we experience, which Covey calls being proactive. He describes the Circle of Concern: all the things we can worry about. Next, the Circle of Influence, which lies inside the Circle of Concern: all those things we can do something about. Proactive people focus on the Circle of Influence and if you can do that, you will diminish the Circle of Concern.

Habit 2: Begin with the end in mind

This chapter starts with a famous invitation to attend our own funeral and listen to what others have to say about us.

We begin many things with the end in mind. We rarely leave the house without a destination – you can't plan the route if you don't know where you are headed. Yet too often, people allow their lives to happen to them, with no destination in mind at all.

If management is doing the thing right, and leadership is about doing the right thing, then be a leader. Figure out the destination for both the big and the small things in life, so that you do not waste time wandering aimlessly and then wondering why you don't achieve as much as you had hoped.

If I interrogate my own life, I do this far too often. Sometimes it's ok: an afternoon spent reading can be productive and healthy. Often not; surfing the internet or spending time on Facebook is usually a waste of good time.

This is also where the phrase "Make a promise and keep it," comes into play. That's integrity, pure and simple, be true to others, but also to yourself.

Beware too of getting stuck in management, rather than leadership, in work and in personal development. It's so much easier to engage in management than in leadership, because you get immediate short-term rewards and progress is motivating. Leadership requires the ability to step back and to think. Yes, it is less rewarding and takes more effort in the short term but it is infinitely more rewarding in the longer term.

Under Habit 2 Covey has long sections on being Principle-Centred and about "using the whole brain". These may resonate with some, but I find them outdated given the advances in our understanding of the brain and our decision-making. We have better models today.

Habit 3: Put first things first

Habit 3 is about managing against the leadership objectives you set in Habit 2. Even if as a CEO you should not be managing others because your job is to lead, you still have to manage yourself.

This is where Covey introduces the Eisenhower Matrix, although he doesn't call it that. I believe this is the most effective time-management tool ever invented.

Here's how Covey beaks down the activities:

	URGENT	NOT URGENT
IMPORTANT	I ACTIVITIES: Crises Pressing Problems Deadline-driven projects	II ACTIVITIES: Prevention, Exercise, Health Relationship Building Recognising new opportunities Planning recreation
NOT IMPORTANT	III ACTIVITIES: Interruption, some calls Some email, some reports Some meetings Proximate pressing matters Popular activities	IV ACTIVITIES: Trivia, busywork Some email Some phone calls Time wasters Pleasant activities

Figure 5: Eisenhower matrix

Part Three – Habits 4-6

You can pretty well summarise .... the next three with 'involve others in the problem and work out the solution together.'
–Stephen Covey

Habits 4-6 are all about what we now call social intelligence: how we interact with others, how we nurture our relationships with others and how we influence others and are influenced by them. Covey uses the same definition of effectiveness that he used in the first three habits: production, P and production capability, PC. In the first three habits you are PC, the goose, and P is what you produce: golden eggs. In the second section P represents the wonderful outcomes of productive relationships, synergy, team spirit, great business results, and PC is the relationships themselves, which need constant nurturing to produce the outputs we all desire.

Covey tells a powerful story about his sons and concludes with a critical lesson: "People are very tender, very sensitive inside. Neither age nor experience make much difference. Inside, even within the most toughened and calloused exteriors, are the tender feelings and emotions of the heart."

He also shares his thinking about what he calls the "emotional bank account". We constantly make deposits and withdrawals into the emotional bank account in our dealings with all our interlocuters. A deposit is a good conversation, a shared joke, or a promise kept. A withdrawal on the emotional bank account is a sharp word, an argument badly managed, or a promise broken.

Another great point that Covey makes is "be loyal to those not present." Too often we forget to stand up for those who are being unfairly commented upon in their absence. Doing so shows up our integrity in a powerful way.

Habit 4 – Win-win or no deal

I love habit 4. Win-Lose stops being an option and your stance becomes win-win or no deal. Habit 4 will make you a better negotiator and, in more modern language than Covey's, will help us engage with setting intentions that focus on better outcomes, rather than on being right or on winning the point. The best way to achieve this is to engage Habit 5.

Habit 5 – Seek first to understand, then to be understood

Perhaps my favourite of the seven. I agree with Covey that we cannot really listen to others until we have a solid base of understanding about ourselves. Perhaps the genius of *The 7 Habits* lies there – in the idea that first we must work on ourselves and only then can we put ourselves aside in order to focus fully and powerfully on others.

Covey was way ahead of his time in Habit 5. The power of listening is one of the fundamentals of all coaching, which was in its infancy when Covey wrote his masterpiece.

I have a business partner who talks a lot. We are well balanced because I listen a lot. Our ways of developing business are diametrically opposed – he's brilliant and very successful, by the way. But I, over the years and with a lot of hard work on my own insecurities, have learned to listen. Not merely to stop talking, but to listen and think, What does this mean? What am I learning about this person?

Learning this skill began many years ago. I was living in the South of France and had quite a serious career. I had also picked up a slot as the Arts Critic on Riviera Radio, the local English language radio station. Every Sunday night I would drive to Monaco, a distance of about 30 kilometres, to sit in a quiet, dark studio, and for 20 or 30 minutes the Sunday night classical music presenter and I would discuss what was happening on the busy Riviera arts scene. As a result, when I went to the theatre, the opera, a concert or an art exhibition, I learned not just to listen, but to listen with great attention, thinking, "What does this mean?" "What is unique and special about this that I can share?" That skill, which I began to learn in my 20s, has been a great asset all my life.

Habit 6 – Synergise

This one is tricky. I am not convinced it is a "habit" as such. Covey says that synergistic meetings and teams achieve extraordinary things. The foundation of such synergy is trust, or, as Covey puts it, "a high emotional bank account" among all those present. But how to create a habit out of this, so that every meeting, every encounter, is synergistic? A lofty ambition, hard to achieve in the gritty day-to-day of business.

The main challenge I see is in that tendency we all have to shift from comfort to defensiveness. If we can learn to manage the "fight, flight or freeze" response in ourselves and in others, we'll have a better chance of achieving synergy. I would suggest too that this is where the red head/blue head approach can be useful[20]. Teach that methodology to the team and you will have better meetings – maybe even synergistic ones. Where I do agree with Covey is when he says that synergy is where the magic happens. When the whole becomes greater than the parts and a combination of brains produces a better result than a single one ever could.

Leading synergistic meetings is all about focusing on the other without losing sight of the end goal. That's highly sophisticated, which is why I would call it a skill rather than a habit, and a skill well worth having.

---

20 See blog on "Self Management", page 30.

Part Four – Habit 7

"Sharpen the saw"

The seventh habit, "sharpen the saw", falls right into the "important, not urgent" quadrant (see Habit 2) where, all too often, it gets neglected. It is a commitment to life-long learning. In my view, learning has never been more important; it's our gateway to being successful, high-contributing humans in the fourth industrial revolution. It's no longer possible to be a technophobe, to neglect attempting to understand blockchain and bitcoin and the other new technologies. Blockchain alone may yet change the world, so it merits further investigation and understanding, as do AI, biochemistry, biotech, robotics, the battle against single-use plastics, and the changes in education needed to deal with all those and so much more.

What's more, our understanding of how humans think, judge and make decisions has evolved in the past 10 to 15 years and it is incumbent on every leader to understand what that means for leadership in a world of talented but distracted millennials. To say nothing of the soon-to-arrive Gen Zedders, who may have spent too much of their short lives looking at screens rather than the world around them.

If, as leaders, we demonstrate a willingness to learn, we will inspire those around us. The challenge is that learning takes work. You simply cannot develop deep learning from Google and YouTube, though both can be excellent starting points. Serious learning requires the reading of books and articles and choosing "credible others" to learn from.

Covey doesn't just talk about learning technology and leadership and management topics. He says that we need to sharpen the saw in four areas:

- Physical
- Mental
- Social/emotional
- Spiritual

Once again, I see Covey as far ahead of his time. He wrote *The 7 Habits* long before Daniel Goleman wrote *Emotional Intelligence* and *Social Intelligence*. At that time, the concept of multiple intelligences was circulating only in academia, driven by Harold Gardener, among others. Covey was really smart to pick up on the importance of these concepts so early on.

Many of my clients fully grasp the importance of investing in our physical wellbeing and understand the benefits physical exercise delivers to the brain. If we exercise, we stay mentally fitter as well as physically fitter; there is little doubt about that now.

Mental saw-sharpening requires an investment in reading and learning, an effort that many CEOs simply don't have time for. Yet, reading good books, or at the very least an occasional copy of the *Harvard Business Review* and *The Economist*, is essential. You need to have a point of view, not just about your business, but about the world.

Social and emotional intelligence require a different kind of development. These are the areas that may benefit most from coaching because you need another brain to work with; an outside influence that can ask good questions, driving deeper reflection on matters you might otherwise avoid. Social and emotional intelligence are the bedrock of great leadership. If you have these, you do not need to be the cleverest person in the room because you will have the ability to pull all the clever brains together and create true synergy.

Spiritual development is something I am less qualified to discuss because I have struggled with it my whole life. Learning about both mindfulness and meditation, and my personal experience, has led me to become more grounded in terms of spiritual development. Meditation in particular is being shown to give us the same kind of brain "reset" as sleep does. In a world where sleep doesn't come easily, that is of huge value. And with more meditation comes better sleep.

Personally, I am really bad at meditation. I forget to do it. I spend much of my meditation time thinking "When will this end?" I've managed a maximum of seven minutes so far. But I keep at it. I know the benefits are real. In a stressful life I can feel how calm my mind is after a few minutes of meditation.[21]

The benefits so far? Sleep and energy. Not exactly what I would call spiritual but I'll take both.

A warning though, best summed up by Covey: "Meditation and your own values can bring peace and spirituality. They can give you what *you* need. But be careful! They don't make you right!"[22]

Covey also quotes Phillip Brooks: "Character cannot be made except by a steady, long, continual process." In my 50s now, I am astonished at how much I am still changing and growing, and I expect now that it will continue throughout my life. When I was in my 20s an Italian professor told me "Don't ever change." (I confess, he was an admirer.) *"Ormai, son fatta* [By now I am made]," I replied. How wrong was I. We are never done with growth and change.

Covey suggests that we should give ourselves a Daily Private Victory. This is an hour a day devoted to renewal of ourselves, in the physical, mental and spiritual dimensions. If we factor in exercise this is not

---

21 See blog on "Meditation", page 57.

22 For more on this, see the "Tony Blair Syndrome" blog, page 19.

unreasonable. A short read, a short run and a few minutes of meditation and that hour is quickly achieved. One of my favourite authors, Arnold Schwarzenegger, points out that we are awake for about 16 hours a day. Even a busy CEO should be able to devote one of those hours to "sharpening the saw".

Part 9

STRANGE TIMES

Motivation and emotion in a time of lockdown[23]

After almost four weeks of lockdown I've started to notice a strange thing. For a person who is highly motivated, and indeed I have finished this book, *Keep Your Focus*, during these weeks, I still find myself strangely lacking in energy and my normal level of productivity.

Speaking to clients, some who are in senior leadership roles are staying focused and engaged. Others are extremely stressed about the uncertainty of the future. Those who are in large, high-contact organisations like food retail and mining are deeply concerned about the possibility of escalating rates of infection and even possible deaths among their employees as the lockdown ends.

As leaders who care greatly for their people, the responsibility weighs heavily at personal level. As 'A-type", high productivity leaders, who are used to managing their emotions, they are finding it difficult to manage their feelings at this time, even though they may find this hard to admit, even to themselves. Some of my clients have admitted to feeling low, almost depressed at times, and to being annoyed with themselves about feeling like that. Opening up about such matters only happens towards the end of a coaching session and it is much harder to make that true connection via Zoom, though we are getting better at it.

Among my broader group of friends, we've talked about how strange it is not to be active and productive. 34 days into lockdown we haven't done things we thought we would do, like watch endless series on Netflix, or read dozens of books. Many have moved into a sort of hibernation mode, where you can't believe it's been five weeks of lockdown already and where did the time go? There's constant worry, in particular for breadwinners, about what the future holds, what's going to happen to

---

23 Written in April 2020, a time of great uncertainty.

the economy, are we going to have jobs to go back to? There is also an endless round of home schooling, cooking, cleaning, trying to work from home that leaves surprisingly little "free" time.

Some friends are in denial. "The lockdown wasn't necessary." "The whole thing is ridiculous". "It's no worse than a bad flu so why have we shut down the economy?" "And anyway, it only affects the old and the compromised, so let them get it and let's not ruin the entire economy for the sake of their lives." Perhaps it feels a bit different when suddenly it's their old people who start to die. That's a shock.

In all of this I see reflections of the cycle of grief. That well-known path of mourning that leads from denial, to anger, depression and finally acceptance. We are grieving the world and the life we have lost, for how long we know not. We will probably cycle through the phases, feeling sad, frustrated, annoyed, irritated, calm, cross, relieved to be safe, scared of the impact and the unknown future.

The strangeness of the shopping experience, the empty roads as we drive to collect essentials. The petrol tank that suddenly seems to last forever. Recovery from grief is not a straight and even road, and dealing with this Coronavirus will be similar. No matter how strong you are, accept your emotions. Grant yourself permission. Sit with the emotions, allow yourself to feel disconsolate, low, angry, to deny the sense of it all. There's no point in dismissing these emotions. They are not going to go away.

What you can do is confront your deepest fears. If you are worrying during the night, or feeling anxious, take the time to write down your fears and to address full on what you can do to prevent the worst from happening. In some cases you may not have control over that, so write down what you will do if the worst does happen. Because fears confronted usually diminish and you may surprise yourself with what you'll come up with as a plan to deal with them.

There's a good Tedtalk by Tim Ferris on Fear of Failure where he describes a clever process to face your fears. Divide a page into three columns. In column 1 make a list of what is worrying you. All of it, no matter how bad. In column 2 write down anything you can do to prevent this thing from happening. In column 3 write down how you will manage if this awful thing does happen and what you will do to fix it. Facing your worst fears, like facing down a bad bully, is the best way to address them.

Here are a couple of mine. I would imagine that many of us have fears like these.

Fear	Prevent	Repair
1. That I will have no business left when this 's over.	Stay close to clients. Don't worry about money now. Be there for them because I care about them as people and they are going through as much as me and more.	When lockdown ends be really disciplined about restarting the business through business development... etc.
2. That my loved ones in Europe, the US, and eventually here in Africa, who are vulnerable will get it and die.	I cannot prevent this. This is beyond my control.	The only thing I can do is stay close family, talk to them regularly, let them know I'm here and I love them. Be there for them.

Fear	Prevent	Repair
3.		
4.		
5.		
6.		
7.		

Part 10

THE LEADERSHIP JOURNEY

The Leadership Journey – the next book

In assessing senior executives for succession planning and career development, I can see that people get stuck on the leadership journey. Remember we talked about being stuck in the bereavement process? Well, being stuck on the leadership journey is the same in many ways.

The Leadership Journey

People can get stuck at any point of the bereavement process and they can bounce around the different phases before reaching true acceptance. The Leadership Journey is not so different. Here is the way I like to break it down:

Level 1: reactive self
Level 2: skills and knowledge acquisition
Level 3: engagement with others
Level 4: work begins on self-mastery
Level 5: driving operational excellence which includes encouraging learning from mistakes
Level 6: growing and developing great talent around you
Level 7: development of social intelligence
Level 8: upskilling of strategy and vision and the ability to communicate both
Level 9: driving empowerment and ownership up and down the chain of command
Level 10: driving strong communications up and down the chain of command
Level 11: stepping back from the detail; entrusting it to others so that you can define the purpose and the future of the business

You might have a high level of competency at one level and a lower one at the next and a solid one at the level above that. I don't believe you can have a high level of competency at one level if you have little or no competency at the level below. Some people are more gifted than others at certain levels. The ability to join the dots and think conceptually enhances strategic thinking. Social intelligence can be learned, but some people have a natural talent for it and instinctively understand the benefits. In both cases the skills can be honed and improved, but natural talent always helps.

The leadership journey is the work of a lifetime – even Peter Drucker did some of his best work after the age of 65. Stephen Covey said he was still working on mastering *The 7 Habits* 20 years after he wrote the book.

Not everyone gets stuck, and not all at the same level, but many are stuck. Great operational skills are a *sine qua non* of business, so many of managers and executives are strong, though not necessarily innovative, at Level 5.

In many years of assessing senior executives I see pockets of excellence, some great individual leaders and some organisations who take Executive Development seriously, but that is rare. Indeed some senior executives never get beyond Level 5, and, they might be struggling with Level 4.

My next book will build on the framework of The Leadership Journey.

CONCLUSION

The 2020 Coronavirus lockdown has given me the time to finish this book. But it is a strange time to write. Living history is hard to pin down on a page and the real impact of what we are living through remains difficult to assess. In a year, or two, we will have a better grasp, of now and of what is yet to come. At this moment, the best analysis I've found comes from Mark Mason in his blog where he rightly says, no-one knows what's going on. Written a month ago in April, it remains true now, in July. Mark wrote the incredibly successful book *The Subtle Art of Not Giving a F**** and he's a great millennial observer and commentator on our times.

I hope that one day I will update this conclusion on a more positive note, when we have moved properly into the recovery phase. Because, I do believe we will recover, but it will take time, it will be painful and not all of us will live to see it.

The themes and tools that I write about in this book are more relevant than ever in a Coronavirus world.

In my leadership work with clients, those who stand out are those who understand, and want to learn more about, the critical importance of self-awareness and the impact of their behaviour on others. These are the people who, I hope, lead us forward.

During my own lockdown I was lucky enough to see this kind of leadership first- hand. Niall Quirk is one of the great dressage trainers of the world and he is one of my oldest friends. He is Irish, like me, and lives in the US. Before the lockdown started he was in Johannesburg training clients, then he came to the Cape to stay with me, and stayed on when the lockdown was announced. Niall is extraordinarily good at coaching, a leader in his field and one who constantly aims to raise his game. He has been at the global forefront of transforming how equestrian skills are taught, both to riders and to coaches.

I was listening to him discuss a new programme for riders as I was considering how to write this conclusion. He was explaining that the vast majority of equestrian athletes are people who work and can only ride perhaps three times a week, at most. Riding is a deeply physical sport and the best way to ride well is to spend many hours in the saddle. If you can't do that, it's hard for your body to stay open and available to your horse. As we sit in front of desks, on planes or in cars we damage the physical capabilities we need most for competitive riding. To solve this, Niall has decided to work with Colette de Vries, a world-class Pilates and movement coach. Their aim is to develop a programme for riders that would bring the fluency and freedom of movement they need when they are in the saddle. But, he said, "they will need to do that work every day, and most people don't have the discipline to do that every day."

Why is it so hard to do what would benefit us the most?

Many argue they don't have the time. I disagree. It's because we lack the discipline. I am the first to raise my hand here. I get a lot done, but I could achieve a lot more if I was more disciplined about my allocation of time, our most precious resource. Stephen Covey talks about the seventh habit, sharpening the saw, investing in yourself and your knowledge and he suggests that we can all find an hour per day to sharpen the saw. If you consider that we sleep on average between 6 to 8 hours per night, he's right. Out of the 16 to 18 remaining hours available EVERY day, we should be able to find one hour to "sharpen the saw".

Executive development is not so very different from sporting development. There are many dimensions we can work on to improve. This short book covers only some of those, but I would be willing to bet that most of us could improve in every single area I discuss in these blogs. David Brailsford, the legendary UK cycling coach, transformed British cycling when he realised that small, incremental improvements in many areas can deliver bigger results than step changes in a single area of focus. Small improvements can make a big difference. The first step to change requires that we open our minds to the idea that we can change and improve. The next step is to commit to those changes.

This book is not intended as a self-improvement or self-help book. Yes, there is some guidance in some of these blogs as to how you can bring about change, but I wrote these pieces to bring knowledge to people who don't have time to read the core literature. If you want to know *how* to introduce change and growth into your life, and how to identify and achieve what you want out of life, my book *Find Your Focus; 5 Steps to Your Best Year Ever* makes an excellent companion to this one.

Leadership, whether in business, in sport, or in self, is a journey. For those of us who want to reach our full potential, we will constantly push our boundaries and seek to improve. And we will continually fall back to our old bad habits and lean into our weaker areas. That's ok – because we are human. That's where the discipline comes in. If we keep repeating the better habit, the better behaviour, it becomes easier. Eventually, the new behaviour should become automatic, because, as they say about neurons in neuroscience, "what fires together, wires together". The classic example is that of driving a car. When you first learn to drive it is really hard to get the coordination right. Many years later you barely have to think at all, so automatic has the act of driving become.

The hard part is that the improvement comes when it's most difficult. When you exercise the benefit comes when the effort is greatest. The last repetitions of a set or the final sprint of the run. That's where the benefit happens. The same is true for learning of any kind – it is the discipline of the repetitions that changes the habit and brings about lasting improvement. Mentally, that discipline is hard for all of us. That's why so few of us are as fit, thin, or successful as we'd like to be.

Research on happiness and satisfaction tells us that while increased success and riches, beyond a certain point, will not make us incrementally *happier*, they can make us ever more *satisfied* with our lives. That's important because it shows that the successful effort to improve ourselves as leaders, colleagues, business people, friends, sportspeople, will be rewarded with a deep and important human emotion: satisfaction. Personally, I find this to be true and it is a great motivator for me. Success and satisfaction only ever follow a tough route of multiple failures and hard work; accepting those is essential to reaping the reward of satisfaction with life.

This is more important than ever in 2020 where mortality and financial losses stare all of us in the face. We will survive these times; we will survive through the quality of our work and the quality of our relationships. We will survive because we try.

LIST OF SOURCES

Amabile, T.M. & Kramer, S.J., 2011. The power of small wins. *Harvard Business Review, 89*(5), pp.70-80.

Arnot, S. 2019. *Find your focus. 5 steps to your best year ever.* Randburg: KR Publishing.

Arnot, S. 2019. Vulnerability. *The Fynbos Blog.* Retrieved from: https://fynbosblog.com

Ashkenas, R. 2011. Speaking up takes courage, candour and confidence. *Harvard Business Review.*

Bello, S.M., 2012. Impact of ethical leadership on employee job performance. *International Journal of Business and Social Science, 3*(11).

Björnberg, A. & Feser, C., 2015. CEO succession starts with developing your leaders. *McKinsey Quarterly, 2*, pp. 1-5.

Brown, B. 2010. The Power of Vulnerability. Tedtalk. Retrieved from: https://www.ted.com/talks/brene_brown_the_power_of_vulnerability?language=en

Bubbs, M., 2019. *Peak: the new science of athletic performance that is revolutionizing sports.* White River Junction, Vermont: Chelsea Green.

Burnett, D., 2016. *Idiot Brain: What Your Head Is Really Up To.* New York: WW Norton & Company.

Cain, S., 2013. *Quiet: The power of introverts in a world that can't stop talking.* New York: Broadway Books.

Carey, D., Dumaine, B., Useem, M. & Zemmel, R., 2018. Why CEOs should push back against short-termism. *Harvard Business Review.*

Chun, J.U., Litzky, B.E., Sosik, J.J., Bechtold, D.C. & Godshalk, V.M., 2010. Emotional intelligence and trust in formal mentoring programs. *Group & Organization Management, 35*(4), pp. 421-455.

Ciampa, D., 2016. After the handshake. *Harvard Business Review, 94*(12), pp. 60-68.

Covey, S.R., 1989. *The 7 Habits of Highly Effective People.* New York: Simon & Schuster.

DiAngelo, R., 2018. *White fragility: Why it's so hard for white people to talk about racism.* Beacon Press.

Díaz-García, C., González-Moreno, A. & José Saez-Martinez, F., 2013. Gender diversity within R&D teams: Its impact on radicalness of innovation. *Innovation, 15*(2), pp. 149-160.

Doidge, N. 2007. *The brain that changes itself: Stories of personal triumph from the frontiers of brain science.* New York: Viking.

Dunsmoor, J.E. & Paz, R., 2015. Fear generalization and anxiety: behavioral and neural mechanisms. *Biological psychiatry*, 78(5), pp. 336-343.

Dutra, A. and Griesedieck, J.E., 2010. Planning for your next CEO. *The McKinsey Quarterly*. Retrieved February 22, p.2010.

Efron, L., 2015. Do you have a culture of fear? Three questions to ask. Retrieved from: https://www.forbes.com/sites/louisefron/2017/09/25/do-you-have-a-culture-of-fear-three-questions-to-ask/#331077781435

Ferriss, T., 2017. *Tribe of Mentors: Short Life Advice from the Best in the World*. Boston, MA: Houghton Mifflin Harcourt.

Ferris, T., 2015. Why you should define your fears instead of your goals. Tedtalk. Retrieved from: https://www.google.com/url?sa=t&rct=j&q=&esrc=s&-source=web&cd=1&cad=rja&uact=8&ved=2ahUKEwiprorqkffoAhXNY-MAKHawVDt0QyCkwAHoECAsQBA&url=https%3A%2F%2Fwww.ted.com%2Ftalks%2Ftim_ferriss_why_you_should_define_your_fears_in-stead_of_your_goals%3Flanguage%3Den&usg=AOvVaw1B84tZY1ZEG-fNZl5j2HYWq

Frankl, V.E., 1985. *Man's search for meaning*. New York: Simon and Schuster.

Frisch, C. and Huppenbauer, M., 2014. New insights into ethical leadership: A qualitative investigation of the experiences of executive ethical leaders. *Journal of Business Ethics*, 123(1), pp. 23-43.

Gardner, H., 1992. *Multiple intelligences*. Minnesota Center for Arts Education, 5, p.56.

Gladwell, M., 2008. *Outliers: The story of success*. New York: Little, Brown.

Goleman, D., 2007. *Social intelligence*. New York: Random House.

Gompers, P. and Kovvali, S., 2018. Diversity Dividend. *Harvard Business Review*.

Harrell, E., 2016. Succession planning: What the research says. *Harvard Business Review*, 94(12), pp. 70-74.

Hill, A.P., Witcher, C.S., Gotwals, J.K. and Leyland, A.F., 2015. A qualitative study of perfectionism among self-identified perfectionists in sport and the performing arts. *Sport, Exercise, and Performance Psychology*, 4(4), p. 237.

Hooijberg, R., & Lane, N. 2016. How boards botch CEO succession. *MIT Sloan Management Review*, 57(4), 14.

Hunt, V., Prince, S., Dixon-Fyle, S. and Yee, L., 2018. Delivering through diversity. *McKinsey & Company Report*. Retrieved April 3, p. 2018.

Horowitz, B. 2019. *What you do is who you are*. New York: Harper Business.

Huffington, A.S. 2016. *The sleep revolution: transforming your life, one night at a time*. New York: Harmony.

Iger, Robert. 2019. *The Ride of a Lifetime*. New York: Random House.

Kahneman, D., 2011. *Thinking, fast and slow*. New York: Macmillan.

Kahneman, D. 2020 *The Knowledge Project*. Episode #68 "Putting your Intuition on Ice". Retrieved from: https://fs.blog/knowledge-project/daniel-kahneman/

Kantor, Rosabeth Moss. 2011. 'Courage in the C-Suite'. *Harvard Business Review*.

Kassam, K. S., Koslov, K. and Mendes, W. B. 2009. 'Decisions Under Distress: Stress Profiles Influence Anchoring and Adjustment', *Psychological Science, 20*(11), pp. 1394–1399.

Kerr, J. 2013. *Legacy: What the All Blacks can teach us about the business of life.* London: Little, Brown Book Group.

Kross, E., Bruehlman-Senecal, E., Park, J., Burson, A., Dougherty, A., Shablack, H., Bremner, R., Moser, J. and Ayduk, O., 2014. Self-talk as a regulatory mechanism: How you do it matters. *Journal of personality and social psychology, 106*(2), p. 304.

Kross, E. and Ayduk, O., 2011. Making meaning out of negative experiences by self-distancing. *Current directions in psychological science, 20*(3), pp. 187-191.

Kuppler, Tim. 2013. "The 8 Clear Signs of a Workplace Culture of Fear". *Human Synergistics International*. Retrieved from: https://www.humansynergistics.com/blog/culture-university/details/culture-university/2013/11/14/the-8-clear-signs-of-a-workplace-culture-of-fear

Jones, R., 2015. What CEOs are afraid of. *Harvard Business Review*.

Lafley, A.G., 2009. What only the CEO can do. *Harvard Business Review, 87*(5), pp. 54-62.

Luby, V., & Edison Stevenson, J. 2016. 7 Tenets of a Good CEO Succession Process. *Harvard Business Review*

Maciejewski, Justin. 2019. 'How the British Army's operations went agile'. Interview with the *McKinsey Quarterly*. Retrieved from: https://www.mckinsey.com/business-functions/organization/our-insights/how-the-british-armys-operations-went-agile

Manson, M., 2016. *The Subtle Art of Not Giving a F* ck: A Counterintuitive Approach to Living a Good Life*. Australia: Macmillan Publishers.

Mather, M. and Lighthall, N. R. 2012. 'Risk and Reward Are Processed Differently in Decisions Made Under Stress', *Current Directions in Psychological Science*, 21(1), pp. 36–41.

Maslow, A.H., 1981. *Motivation and personality*. New Delhi: Prabhat Prakashan.

Maxwell, J. C., 2000. *Failing forward: turning mistakes into stepping stones for success*. Nashville, TN: Thomas Nelson.

McLean, B., 2017. How Wells Fargo's cutthroat corporate culture allegedly drove bankers to fraud. *Vanity Fair*.

Menkes, J., 2006. Executive intelligence: What all great leaders have. *Management Today*, *22*(9), pp. 16-22.

Molinsky, A., 2016. Everyone suffers from impostor syndrome – here's how to handle it. *Harvard Business Review*. Retrieved from: https://hbr. org/product/everyone-suffers-from-impostor-syndrome--heres-how-to-handle-it/H02ZSC-PDF-ENG.

Pabst, S., Schoofs, D., Pawlikowski, M., Brand, M., & Wolf, O. T. 2013. Paradoxical effects of stress and an executive task on decisions under risk. *Behavioral Neuroscience, 127*(3), 369–379.

Peppercorn, S. 2018. How to Overcome Your Fear of Failure. *Harvard Business Review*

Peters, S. 2013. The Chimp Paradox: The Mind Management Program to Help You Achieve Success, Confidence, and Happiness. London: Penguin.

Pfeffer, Jeffrey. 2011. "CEOs need Courage". *Harvard Business Review*.

Price, C. and Toye, S., 2017. *Accelerating Performance: How Organizations Can Mobilize, Execute, and Transform with Agility*. New Jersey: John Wiley & Sons.

Reingold, J. 2016. *P&G Chairman A.G. Lafley Steps Down – For Good, This Time*. Retrieved from: https://fortune.com/2016/06/01/pg-chairman-a-g-lafley-steps-down-for-good-this-time/

Ryan, L. 2018. 'Ten unmistakable signs of a fear-based workplace'. Retrieved from: https://www.forbes.com/sites/lizryan/2018/06/23/ten-unmis-takable-signs-you-took-the-wrong-job/#5e58c2837935

Seay, R. 2018. 'What HR Can Do About a Fear-Based Culture'. *Talent Management and HR*. Retrieved from: https://www.tlnt.com/what-hr-can-do-about-a-fear-based-culture/

Sims, P. 2012. The No. 1 Enemy of Creativity: Fear of Failure. *Harvard Business Review*.

Sinek, S., 2009. *Start with why: How great leaders inspire everyone to take action*. London: Penguin.

Smart, G., & Street, R. 2008. *Who? The A method for hiring*. New York: Ballantine Books.

Spangenberg, H. and Theron, C.C., 2005. Promoting ethical follower behaviour through leadership of ethics: The development of the ethical leadership inventory (ELI). *South African Journal of Business Management, 36*(2), pp. 1-18.

Sperling, Julia. 2018. 'Brain researcher takes on bias'. *McKinsey Quarterly*. Retrieved from: https://www.mckinsey.com/about-us/new-at-mck-insey-blog/brain-researcher-takes-on-bias

Stulberg, B. & Magness, S., 2017. *Peak Performance: Elevate Your Game, Avoid Burnout, and Thrive with the New Science of Success.* Pennsylvania: Rodale Books.

The Economist. 2016. 'The Outside Track'. Retrieved from: https://www.economist.com/business/2016/04/23/the-outside-track

The Economist. 2019. 'How to make your firm more diverse and inclusive'. Retrieved from: https://www.economist.com/business/2019/11/07/how-to-make-your-firm-more-diverse-and-inclusive

Tiefenthaler, I., 2018. Conquering Imposter Syndrome. *University of Montana Journal of Early Childhood Scholarship and Innovative Practice, 2*(1), p. 4.

Todd, S., 2018. Uber's IPO is a lesson in the true cost of toxic culture. *Quartz at Work.* Retrieved from: https://qz.com/work/1593845/the-uber-ipo-filing-admits-workplace-culture-is-a-risk-factor/

Turunç, Ö., Çelik, M. and Mert, İ.S., 2013. The impact of leadership styles on ethical behaviour. *Journal of Academic Research in Economics, 5*(1).

Webb, C. 2016. *How to Have A Good Day: The essential toolkit for a productive day at work and beyond.* London: Pan Macmillan.

Wilber, K., 2000. *Integral psychology: Consciousness, spirit, psychology, therapy.* Boston, MA: Shambhala Publications.

Willink, J. & Babin, L., 2017. *Extreme ownership: How US Navy SEALs lead and win.* New York: St. Martin's Press.

Willink, J. & Babin, L., 2018. *The dichotomy of leadership: balancing the challenges of extreme ownership to lead and win.* New York: St. Martin's Press.

Zwilling, M. 2018. 'How to change the culture of an organisation that's managed by fear'. Retrieved from: https://www.inc.com/martin-zwilling/5-ways-to-recognize-if-your-team-is-managed-by-fear-what-you-can-do-about-it.html

INDEX

V

values and principles, 94
values and standards, 89, 91
vulnerability, 6, 11–12

W

wellbeing, 51, 70, 96, 104
women in leadership, 45

www.ingramcontent.com/pod-product-compliance
Lightning Source LLC
Chambersburg PA
CBHW071909200326
41519CB00016B/4542